NEW MEXICO

JOURNEY GUIDE

A DRIVING & HIKING GUIDE TO RUINS, ROCK ART, FOSSILS & FORMATIONS

WRITTEN BY JON KRAMER AND JULIE MARTINEZ
ILLUSTRATIONS BY VERNON MORRIS

Adventure Publications
Cambridge, Minnesota

Authors' Dedications

To my sister Thecla Diane, who has consistently encouraged me in the pursuit of this adventurous life, whose dedication to family is deeply appreciated, and whose love of the Southwest is infectious. And, as always, to my incredible wife who continually astounds me and whose love guides me.

–JON KRAMER

To all the people in my life who encouraged me to look through binoculars, pick up a worm, or chase a butterfly. And, as always, to my wonderful husband, life companion and fellow explorer Jon.

–JULIE MARTINEZ

To the ancient people who built and inhabited the ruins, pecked their artwork into stone, and scouted the trails we follow today.

–VERN MORRIS

The authors would like to express gratitude and special thanks to those who treat the Earth and all its creatures with the reverence and respect they deserve. The Great Spirit smiles upon you each sunrise.

Special thanks to Dave Bunnell for reviewing the book.

Photo credits by artist and page number:
Cover photos by Jon Kramer, Julie Martinez and Vernon Morris: Pecos National Historical Park (main photo), La Cieneguilla Petroglyphs (left inset), Coelophysis skeleton (middle inset) and Three Rivers Petroglyphs (right inset)
All photos copyright Jon Kramer, Julie Martinez and Vernon Morris unless otherwise noted.
Richard Anderson: 198, **Dave Bunnell:** 72 **Ray Colby:** 16, 22, 32, 34 (both), 36, 39 (upper right), 40, 41, 42 (both), 46 (top), 49, 54, 56 (both), 64, 66 (bottom), 80, 85 (both), 92, 96 (top right), 137 (top), 156 (top), 157, 176, 178 both), 179, 182, 190, 200, 202 (both), 203 **Sally King/National Park Service:** 44

Artwork credits by artist and page number:
Julie Martinez: 9, 11, 12, 14, 15 **Vernon Morris**: 12, 22, 26, 31, 43, 48, 67, 95, 101, 121, 123, 133, 141, 161

Edited by Brett Ortler
Cover and book design by Jonathan Norberg

10 9 8 7 6 5 4
New Mexico Journey Guide
Copyright © 2009 by Jon Kramer, Julie Martinez and Vernon Morris
Published by Adventure Publications
An imprint of AdventureKEEN
310 Garfield Street South
Cambridge, Minnesota 55008
(800) 678-7006
www.adventurepublications.net
All rights reserved
Printed in China
ISBN 978-1-59193-221-5 (pbk.)

Special Thanks

When I was growing up in the D.C. metro area, our family lived in an apartment complex that was managed by our mother. I had a friend named Mike who lived in the same building and his folks became good friends with my own. Mike and I were forever the sarcastic practical jokers, stealing each other's stuff and sabotaging things. But we did have some good energy together. Among our favorite hobbies was engineering improbably fast, one-person, 3 or 4-wheeled speed-vehicles cobbled together from borrowed shopping carts and old bikes. These we would race down the hill of the parking lot beside our building—sans brakes (brakes don't exist in a 12-year-old's plans). In our enthusiasm, it did not occur to us that residents driving a car through the crowded lot had little chance of seeing the demon kids of Building 12 flying downhill in their low-slung contraptions. Oftentimes we would skid around a corner, squealing directly into the path of on-coming tires. It is nothing short of a miracle that we lived through those years of haphazard vehicular experimentation with nary a scratch.

As we grew, life took Mike and I along different paths. We stayed in touch primarily through our parents, who had become excellent, life-long friends. Eventually we somehow adopted each other's parents and would visit them when the opportunity arose. Although he landed in Indiana, Mike's parents moved to Albuquerque and for the last 20 years I've seen a lot more of them then I have of Mike himself. They've always had the door open and the light on for the "roving band of adventurers" that would crash at their home, empty the refrigerator, and destroy the washing machine. We cannot begin to thank Joe, Nancy, and Maggie Jolly enough for their kindness and warmth. Their home has always been a welcome haven. Mike, on the other hand, would do well to relinquish my bike light which he has held captive for some 20 or so years. Don't make me come to Indiana, Mike—I'm warning you!

On a recent visit to Acoma Pueblo, I found myself atop the mesa in that most-embarrassing of modern shopping scenarios where I had contracted to purchase a hand-beaded bracelet for my wife but had not a single cent on me with which to complete the transaction. To the rescue came a couple on the same tour—Mike and Sally—who lent me the cash until we got back to the cars. But it doesn't end there! My calamity was compounded when, on the way back down, it occurred to me I had already spent my last few dollars on some Navajo bread (yummy indeed, and well worth it) in Zuni. I confessed to the poor folks I did not, in fact, have any cash to repay them. But by the time we got to the cars I was able to offer up the only thing I could think of in trade—a copy of the **Arizona Journey Guide**. They loved it. More importantly, Julie loves the bracelet. The ancient system of bartering lives on . . .

Say you are writing a guidebook but are not much of a photographer. If you want good photos there are two ways to go about it: 1) Take a zillion photos of the same subject until you accidentally get a nice one worth publishing or, 2) Hire a professional. Lucky for us, and you, there is a third choice in this particular case. Ray Colby, both good friend and disciple of the cause, accompanied us to New Mexico these last few years. More importantly, Ray is a professional photographer (www.RayColby.com) whose talents are apparent on several of these pages. We appreciate it and are sure you will also.

TABLE OF CONTENTS

Welcome to New Mexico 6

Keep in Touch 7

Using This Guide 8

  About the Listings 8

  Map and key 9

  Ratings 10

  Access 11

  Museums 11

Introducing New Mexico 12

  Archaeology 12

  Paleontology 14

  Geology 15

Visitor Etiquette 17

  Irreplaceable Treasures 17

  Do Not Disturb 17

  Wilderness Areas 17

Precautions 18

  Bring Lots of Water 18

  The Big Chill 18

  Rock Fall 18

  Snowstorms 19

  Flash Floods 19

  Roads 19

  Dust storms 20

  Animals 20

Plants 21

The Best of New Mexico 22

Archaeology–Chaco Culture National Historical Park 22

Paleontology–Clayton Lake State Park 22

Geology–Carlsbad Caverns National Park 23

The Sites, A-Z 24

Museums 220

References and Websites 223

Glossary 224

Index 228

About the Authors 232

Welcome to New Mexico

South of Jacksonville, Florida there's a quaint historic seaside town called St. Augustine. It's fairly old as towns in the U.S. go, having been established in 1565, forty years before the founding of Jamestown. St. Augustine likes to call itself "The Nation's Oldest City"—a promotional jingle which is trumpeted endlessly throughout town and splashed across the city's official website.

But there's a hitch: St. Augustine isn't the oldest city in the country. There are many older by far. If you want proof, just head to New Mexico.

Now, don't get me wrong, I love St. Augustine. The people are cool and the place is cosmo. It's just that if you were to press the "Truth in Advertising" issue, the town council would have to come up with some-

thing more like: "St. Augustine—the oldest, more-or-less continuously-inhabited city in the U.S. founded by Europeans, excluding those in the Southwest." Admittedly it's a bit cumbersome—a veritable pig-iron phrase —so I wouldn't expect it to be adopted anytime soon.

The point is, if you really want to see old cities on this continent, head to the Southwest. Here, in New Mexico and the other 4-corner states, you'll find a number of places which blow away anything in the East. Take, for example, Bandelier National Monument. There's conclusive evidence this area was peopled over 10,000 years ago. Ever heard of Chaco Canyon? Its rip-roaring party was in full swing 600 years before anyone even thought about landing in the "New World." And then there's Acoma and Taos Pueblos—two towns that have been continually occupied for well over 1,000 years and are thriving today.

So the next time you're kicking back with your spouse, neighbor, or a visiting space alien, and they say something like "Let's check out St. Augustine—it's the oldest city in America!" you might be inclined to set the record straight. Then take off to New Mexico and visit some of the sites we list here. You'll find truly old cities and have tremendous fun exploring "The Land of Enchantment."

Now there's a slogan that rings true.

JourneyGuides.com

Jon, Julie, & Vern

Keep In Touch

After you've been through a few of these places, why not do us a favor and drop us a line? We really do want to hear how things went. Did you find our little book here useful? Did it give you a good idea of what to expect? How can we make it better? Or maybe you're mad as a hornet because your car got stuck trying to get to San Lorenzo Canyon (I told you to call ahead!) and you want to vent? Well—go ahead and fire away, let us have it: the good, the bad, and the ugly. We want to hear it all.

Or perhaps you've seen some incredible sites that deserve to be in a guide like this? Let us know and we'll check it out. If we use it in the next edition, you'll get credited and we'll send you a gift as well. So keep in touch . . .

Email us via: **JourneyGuides.com**

or, write us at:

New Mexico Journey Guide
c/o Adventure Publications
820 Cleveland St. S.
Cambridge, MN 55008

Using This Guide

About the listings

When you glance at this map the first thing you think is—"What's with the site numbers scattered all over the place?" Now take it easy, there's a reason: All the sites are in alphabetical order by name. So, naturally, they do not follow any sort of geography. Every site we list—be it on private, public, or reservation land—is open to the public as of the date of this printing. But things change and it's always good to confirm ahead of time by phone.

SITE NUMBER		PAGE NUMBER
1	Abo Ruin	25
2	Acoma Pueblo (Sky City)	29
3	Angel Peak Scenic Area	33
4	Aztec Arches	37
5	Aztec Ruins National Monument	41
6	Bandelier National Monument	45
7	Bandera Volcano and Ice Cave	51
8	Bisti/De-Na-Zin Wilderness	55
9	Blue Hole	59
10	Bottomless Lakes State Park	61
11	Capulin Volcano National Monument	65
12	Carlsbad Caverns National Park	69
13	Casamero Pueblo Ruins	75
14	Catwalk National Scenic Trail	77
15	Chaco Culture National Historical Park	81
16	City of Rocks State Park	89
17	Clayton Lake State Park	93
18	Coronado State Monument	99
19	Echo Amphitheater	103
20	El Malpais National Monument	105
21	El Morro National Monument	111
22	Fort Stanton Recreation Area	115
23	Ghost Ranch	119
24	Gila Cliff Dwellings National Monument	123
25	Gran Quivira	129

SITE NUMBER		PAGE NUMBER
26	Jemez Falls and McCauley Hot Springs	135
27	Jemez State Monument	139
28	Kasha-Katuwe Tent Rocks National Monument	143
29	La Cieneguilla Petroglyphs	147
30	Ojito Wilderness	151
31	Orilla Verde Recreation Area	155
32	Pecos National Historical Park	159
33	Petroglyph National Monument	165
34	Poshuouinge Ruins	169
35	Purgatory Chasm	171
36	Quarai Ruin	173
37	Red Rock Park	177
38	Rockhound State Park & Spring Canyon	181
39	Salmon Ruins and Heritage Park	183
40	San Lorenzo Canyon	187
41	Shiprock	191
42	Simon Canyon Ruin	193
43	Sitting Bull Falls and Cave	195
44	Soda Dam	199
45	Taos Pueblo	201
46	Three Rivers Petroglyph Site	205
47	Tome Hill	209
48	Valley of Fires Recreation Area	213
49	White Sands National Monument	217

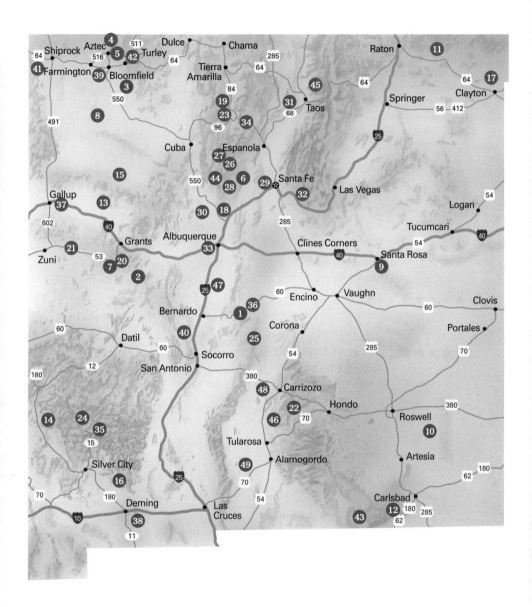

Shiprock
64
Aztec **4**
Farmington **41**
5
516
511
Turley **42**
64
Dulce
Chama
285
Tierra 64
Amarilla
84
Bloomfield **39**
3
550
Raton
11
64
Springer
64
Clayton
17
56 — 412
8
491
Cuba
19
23
96
34
31
68
Taos
45
45
15
Gallup
37
602
13
Espanola
27
26
44 **6**
550 **28**
29 ☆ Santa Fe
32
30 **18**
285
Las Vegas
Logan
54
Tucumcari
40
Grants
40
Zuni
53
21
7 **20**
2
Albuquerque
33
Clines Corners
40
Santa Rosa
9
25
47
Bernardo
1 **36**
Encino
60
Vaughn
60
Clovis
60
Corona
60
Portales
70
Datil
40
60
Socorro
25
54
285
70
180
12
San Antonio
380
48 Carrizozo
Hondo
380
14
24
35
15
22
46 70
Roswell
10
Tularosa
Silver City
16
49
70
Alamogordo
Artesia
180
62 180
70
180
Deming
10
38
11
Las
Cruces
54
Carlsbad
43
12 180 285
62

Ratings

In the rating of each entry we give you an idea of the quality of experience you can expect with that aspect of the site. Our ratings are, admittedly, subjective. You may not agree with what we think all the time but you'll get the hang of it. The ratings are determined by our own personal standards. For the record, we take into account the quality and quantity of the subject matter, its educational value and presentation, and our overall impression of the experience visiting the site. We use a scale of 1–5 stars with some plus or minus for in-betweens. Like in the hotel trade, five stars is top honors. Here's an approximation of how we rate things:

★☆☆☆☆   B-O-R-I-N-G and/or barely worthy of note, but for some reason we listed it anyway. Don't waste your time by going out of the way to see this one.

★★☆☆☆   Stop here if you're in the area and need to kill time. Who knows, you may like it more than the rating suggests.

★★★☆☆   Definitely worth a visit, no excuse necessary. Even if it means going a little off course to see it.

★★★★☆   This place warrants a detour and/or change of plans to visit although you might want to stop short of divorcing your partner to get here.

★★★★★   Shazzam! This site is worthy of quitting your job and hitchhiking cross-country just to catch a glimpse of it. Go ahead, divorce your spouse if you need to—it's worth it!

Access

The ease with which you can access the main aspects of each location is indicated in a generalized way. Do not take this as gospel! Remember, you are responsible for your own well-being. Things change all the time, especially in the no-man's land of some of these places. Check beforehand with local land managers if you have any question about the difficulty. (And by the way, we've included the contact information so you can't complain to us about not knowing whom to call for a road and trail condition report). In some cases, we indicate the difficulty of access by car to the trail head versus the difficulty of the trail itself. Trail ratings are loosely defined along these lines:

Easy
No real problem. The site has parking nearby or within a short, easy walk. If there are any complaints, you've taken the wrong path.

Moderate
Usually requires some hiking over moderate topographic relief. No need for swearing and little-to-no sweat.

Difficult
Prolonged and/or rough hiking over significant topographic relief. There's likely to be some sweating here and the trek may occasionally warrant foul language.

Extreme
Very difficult, often multi-day hiking among rugged, remote terrain. Use of foul language and inappropriate gestures probable. Requires profuse sweating under arduous circumstances. Use deodorant.

Many places have multiple sites, some easy to access and others downright extreme. Such places will have a range of ratings that apply. For instance, Bandelier has an Access rating of Easy–Very Difficult. A short tour of the closest ruins is easy. If, however, you wish to hike way back in to remote places, then you're in for more of a challenge.

Museums

We've made a noble effort to inform you of all the natural history museums in the state. Keep in mind we do not attempt to list every single museum found in New Mexico. We have not, for example, informed you about the International UFO Museum and Research Center as spell-binding as it may be, simply because it is not applicable to the type of journey you are on here. The museums we do include are notable educational institutions related to our listings in Archaeology, Paleontology, and Geology.

Archaeology

Some of the most famous archaeology in the world is in New Mexico, but a large portion of it is out of reach of the common everyday enthusiast. Here we've listed only the publicly-accessible archaeology sites in the state at the time of printing. We don't, however, attempt to document *every single site* you might be able to visit if you had 3 weeks, Ironman endurance, a tanker-load of water, and a dedicated chuck wagon. After all, the vast majority of archaeology sites have yet to be documented and many of these are on public land. But we do list those which a normal everyday traveler *can access in one day with reasonable effort in decent weather*.

We will not attempt to educate you on all the ins and outs of the various waves of human influence, occupation, and cultures which play a role in the natural history of this state. Suffice it to say, the list is long and very diverse. The archaeology here, like it is everywhere, is in a constant state of revision, with new sites and new theories being discovered almost weekly. But researchers generally agree on the basic major Pre-Columbian cultural influences in New Mexico and those are shown in the table on the next page.

Note on discovering new sites: If you happen to come across what you think may be a new archaeology site, please do not disturb anything. Take photos, note the exact location on your map or GPS, and notify the Office of the State Archaeologist. Your reward is knowing you did the right thing. Also, consider this added bonus: by virtue of doing nothing at such a site you avoid jail time and bad publicity. Archaeology sites—including rock art—are very strictly protected by law.

APPROXIMATE CHRONOLOGY OF PRE-COLUMBIAN CULTURES IN NEW MEXICO
(using revised Pecos classification)

Cultures in the New Mexico area	Pueblo V	2000
		1900
		1800
		1700
		1600
	Pueblo IV	1500
		1400
		1300
	Pueblo III	1200
		1100
	Pueblo II	1000
		900
	Pueblo I	800
		700
	Basketmaker III	600
		500
		400
		300
		200
		100 AD
		0
	Basketmaker II	100 BC
		200
		300
		400
		500
		600
		700
		800
		900
		1000
Cultures in all of North America		2000
	Archaic	3000
		4000
		5000
		6000
		7000
	PaleoIndian	8000
		9000
		10,000
		11,000

Paleontology

Paleontology sites on public land are also protected by laws, although the exact details and applications thereof are yet being refined by the authorities, most of whom don't know a fossil from a turnip. New Mexico, like many states in the West, is rich with fossils. Its most famous are, of course, the dinosaurs. New Mexico has the honor of being the site of discovery for the largest dinosaurs ever excavated—huge sauropods named *Seismosaurus* and *Ultrasaurus*. These giants have been excavated mainly from the Ojito Wilderness area north of Albuquerque.

Understandably, the rules governing fossil collecting on public land are designed to keep the activity under control. All one has to do is look at the devastation in some areas, such as certain fossil fish sites in southern Wyoming, to see the wholesale destruction wrought by unregulated collecting and basic human greed. There are places which look more like a moonscape than a fossil site.

So before you run off, pick and shovel in hand, to dig merrily for fossils on government land you must first check with the local land management agency to determine exactly what you can and cannot do. For fossil vertebrates, a permit is always required when digging them on federal lands and on most state lands as well. In the case of invertebrates, plants,

and trace fossils, you MAY be allowed to dig some small amount so long as it is for personal, noncommercial use. However in ALL cases you must check in advance with the appropriate authorities for what is, and is not, allowed in the particular area you will be visiting.

Private land, of course, is another matter altogether. The law is clear here: Fossils on private land belong to the land owner. You may dig to your paleontological heart's content on private land so long as you have a contract and/or permission from the owner. And if you happen to own land where fossils outcrop, you can even commercialize your find by charging other enthusiasts a fee to dig them. So get out there and look for a T-rex on your land—it could be worth a few cases of Crown Royal!

Seek Professional Help—Regardless of what you find, keep notes with the specimens as to where exactly they were unearthed and any particulars that may be of interest to researchers. Half the fun of finding a fossil is learning more about it. We strongly encourage you to join a rock club. It's also a good idea to ally yourself with a professional paleontologist in your area, who can help you in learning about your discoveries. In exchange, you might be able to help him/her with their research. It's a win-win situation when we all work together to advance science.

Geology

The single most important geologic "event" in New Mexico is the Rio Grande Rift. As the name suggests, a giant rift valley extends along most of the length of the Rio Grande river, starting as a narrow fracture zone in central Colorado and widening consistently as you follow the river south through New Mexico. At Albuquerque the rift is about 32 miles wide. Starting about 30 million years ago, the Earth's crust began tearing apart along this seam—a process which continues, albeit quiescently, to this day. Episodic volcanism has been associated with the rifting; one excellent example is the Capulin Volcano.

	Years (millions)
CENOZOIC ERA	
Holocene Epoch	
Pleistocene Epoch	
	2
Pliocene Epoch	
	5
Miocene Epoch	
	24
Oligocene Epoch	
	35
Eocene Epoch	
	55
Paleocene Epoch	
MESOZOIC ERA	65
Cretaceous Period	
	140
Jurassic Period	
	200
Triassic Period	
PALEOZOIC ERA	240
Permian Period	
	290
Carboniferous Period	
	360
Devonian Period	
	410
Silurian Period	
	440
Ordovician Period	
	500
Cambrian Period	
PRECAMBRIAN	570
Proterozoic Eon	
	2500
Archean Eon	
	3600
Hadean Eon	
	4500

New Mexico is blessed with a great diversity of geologic provinces, land-forms, and outcrops. Nearly everywhere you look in this state there are unique and exciting geologic features, from the weird, wonderful towers of Tent Rocks to the hoodoos of Ojito. Because a large portion of the state is public land, you're welcome to explore many of the wonders of this geologic cornucopia. But let's face it, even in a dozen volumes, there wouldn't be enough room to describe all the great geology here. So we're gonna take the easy way out and only discuss the highlights which are fairly accessible to you. Keep in mind all the archaeology and paleontology sites have some sort of geologic aspect to them, so even if you don't see mention of them in the listing, you'll doubtless enjoy the added geo-bonus free of charge.

Visitor Etiquette

Irreplaceable Treasures

We're quite sure you don't need to be told that the sites you'll visit are fragile, irreplaceable, natural treasures. We're also certain you don't want to hear again and again that these sites need your care in preserving them. And, really, why would we want to use valuable print space to tell you how important it is for you to take an interest in conserving these sites for future generations when we all know you understand and practice that already? What with all those laws and societal taboos in place to ward off destructive behavior, who in their right mind would even consider such negligence? Certainly not you or us. But you never know. You may come across someone who doesn't understand these things—say a social deviant, or a human with the intelligence of a brick. If you do, you can just show them this paragraph and try to set them on the straight and narrow path. God smiles on those who help preserve the Earth.

Do Not Disturb

Let's suppose you stumble across a huge pile of broken pottery or a petrified log weathered into thousands of fragments at a place not mentioned in this or any other guidebook. You might reason that pocketing just one tiny piece or two couldn't possibly impact the site as a whole, considering the uncountable abundance still left undisturbed, right? No, not right. In fact, VERY not right. If every visitor took just one tiny piece then soon there would be nothing left except an empty hole where once there was a dinosaur skeleton or a cliff dwelling. So please don't do it, don't disturb any sites. Future generations will thank you. And you'll be doing your part in relieving overcrowded prisons by not becoming an inmate.

Wilderness Areas

On the surface of it, designating certain places as "wilderness" may seem like a bureaucratic maneuver designed primarily to cash in on pork-barrel politics. Once you visit them it's not really necessary for someone to remind you of the fact that the place is wilderness to the core. There's often little in the way of improvements—the whole idea of wilderness is a lack of such things. And, the best part is you're not likely to encounter Paris Hilton or Rush Limbaugh schlepping a pack through the remote canyons of such places. However, as redundant as it may seem, wilderness areas do require special consideration because of their fragile nature. The BLM and Park Service have adopted a special idiom in such areas called "Leave No Trace." It's a good policy wherever you travel but is especially important in wilderness areas. The idea is exactly what it says—please try to leave no trace of your passing through such areas. Visit www.LNT.org to learn more.

Precautions

Bring Lots of Water

Most of New Mexico is generally arid. Weather-wise it can be hot or cold depending on where you go and when. In the lowlands, things can get downright sizzling during the day, especially from May–September. The oft-heard "But it's a dry heat!" is little consolation when the mercury zooms past 110 degrees. Bring plenty of drinking water, even in winter. Many of these sites are remote and have no water supply. Here's a lesson in common desert-traveler sense: just because a site is named something provocative like "Crystal Spring" doesn't mean there's a spring there. Or, if there is, it may be an undrinkable slime mold. Also, we've jumped onto the Better Health Bandwagon and are promoting a reduction in skin cancer, so stock up on sunscreen and wear a wide-brim hat. Sunscreen, a hat, and sun glasses are imperative any-time in the mountains.

The Big Chill

If you're camping in the desert, be aware that it can get chilly at night, even in the summer. In the winter, the higher elevations and plateaus can become veritable deep freezes with temps below zero not uncommon. And don't forget the wind! The wind can become a major force to be reckoned with, especially if it's cold. As they say in Minnesota— "Bring warm clothes!"

Rock Fall

Remember that story in 2003 about Aron Ralston, the explorer who was climbing through a Utah canyon when a loose boulder shifted and pinned him against the wall? He was trapped for days before he finally did the

unthinkable and cut off his own arm with a pocket knife so he could escape. He made it out alive, but just barely.

In the wilds, the dynamics of weathering insure a continual supply of loose rock and precariously balanced boulders, especially in the mountains. We recommend you do not tempt fate by scrambling around outside established routes. If you do take the path less traveled, be sure to hike with a companion. We want you to come home with all your limbs intact and with stories a little less harrowing than Aron's. Keep in mind that steep, mountainous terrain can be host to major rockslides, especially during spring thaws.

Snowstorms

If you travel in the higher elevations in winter, be aware that snowstorms can come on fast and furious. Just keep an eye out and stay tuned to the weather. Don't go into remote regions without the right vehicle, reliable equipment, and proper preparation. This is especially true in the winter.

Flash Floods

Do not enter any canyon, creek, river, or wash if there is a chance of rain in the region. Read that last sentence again and pick up on the word "region"—meaning not just the immediate area, but anyplace within the watershed of your area. This is especially important in narrow canyons during spring runoff or during major thunderstorms.

Roads

A great many of the sites we list are accessible by pavement and/or maintained gravel roads. Many others are attained via unimproved dirt tracks that can be dicey in bad weather, even for 4WD. We strongly recommend you check locally about road conditions before heading out to remote sites. If you don't, you may be in for a long hike out and enormous tow-truck charges. Most of these sites do not need 4WD but be sure to use caution anywhere the road is unmaintained.

Dust Storms

If you've lived in a big city all your life you'll no doubt find it highly amusing that dust storms actually do exist. That is, until you're caught in a bad one that lasts hours on end, has ZERO visibility, and permeates everything with a fine-powder grit that takes several washes to get out. Hopefully you won't ever have to endure such a freak of nature but if it happens there's not much you can do about it. If you're driving, pull over. If you're hiking, just hunker down and ride it out. At least you'll have something amusing to tell the folks back home.

Animals

Most of the time you won't encounter bothersome animals. Even if you do, pay attention to some simple rules of thumb and you're not likely to have a problem with them:

- Never, EVER! feed the wildlife. You've heard it before but we'll tell you again: Feeding wildlife encourages dependency on unnatural food sources and may lead to unwanted advances—advances which may not end when you want them to.

- Don't approach wild animals—observe and record them from a distance.

- Live with compassion—and enjoy, but do not harass, other living things. This a good principle applicable to animals as well as plants. It should be observed by people as well as governments. Although it's often ignored by the latter, we hope you, at least, take the message to heart. Even the tarantulas of Chaco Canyon (they love ruins too!) are an important part of the environment, so please drive around them when you see one on the road (they like warm pavement on cold mornings).

No matter where you go or when, we strongly recommend you research the area you are traveling to in order to become familiar with the wildlife you'll encounter. Here is a short list of animals which you should be aware of in New Mexico: mountain lions, wolves, coyotes, bobcats, and javelinas are just a few of the mid-size mammals that can, if necessary, inflict real pain on humans. Just follow the rules above and you're likely to avoid this. Bears don't care much for people and you can

avoid them by keeping your camp clean and food stored properly in your vehicle or bear locker. Elk are obviously huge mammals that can plow you down with little or no reason—don't give them one. Even deer can be lethal. Also, in the summer months, certain other critters come out to play: scorpions, tarantulas, rattlesnakes, Gila monsters, and bees are potentially harmful to humans. Remember, you are just a visitor in their world, so tread softly. Keep an eye out—don't put your hands or feet where you cannot see them, especially under rocks or in crevasses. With a little common sense we can all get along.

Plants

Plants of the desert are another matter altogether. Cactus are ubiquitous throughout much of the state's lowlands and even in the high parks. Be careful where you tread. DO NOT sit on the ground without first checking the spot or you may find yourself asking a travel partner for some unsavory help. (This is exactly what happened to me and it wasn't any fun.) Maintain a bit of distance from cactus and you'll be fine.

The Best of New Mexico

If you had to choose just one site from each category that was the absolute top of its class, which would it be? The following are our choices for the best of the best of New Mexico:

Archaeology

As you can guess, there are some incredible archaeology sites in New Mexico. The problem is picking one place which best represents the diversity and quality of the archaeological experience. The runner-up spot in the competition has to be Gila Cliff Dwellings. But the winner, not surprisingly, is **Chaco Culture National Historical Park**, a place where the volume and diversity of ruins is overwhelming.

Paleontology

New Mexico has an incredible fossil record. There are many superb prehistoric specimens—from dinosaurs to mammoths—which have been unearthed here. The problem is there're not many places in this state

where you can see fossils in the ground. The fossils get dug up as fast as they're noticed. With that in mind, I submit the best public paleo site in the state is **Clayton Lake State Park**. Here you can walk among hundreds of fantastic dinosaur footprints and trackways. This is a rare treat and you should take full advantage of it.

Geology

Now I have a real problem—New Mexico is loaded with awesome geology. It's a tough thing to pick out just one place. Take, for example, "Tent Rocks." From the geologic perspective, that's got to rank as one of the absolute best hikes you'll ever experience. And then there's El Malpais, a truly weird and wild moonscape. But the rule is we can only pick one site to be the Best of New Mexico Geology, so **Carlsbad Caverns National Park** it is. In my opinion it holds the most amazing geology you'll see in New Mexico. It's deep, it's big, and it's world famous (with good reason). If there is only one hole in the ground you see in your entire life, make it this one.

ABO RUIN

Directions: Abo is part of the Salinas Pueblo Missions National Monument. From Mountainair, follow US 60 west approximately 10 miles to the entrance road on the right. The visitor center is less than a mile further on the paved road. If you miss it, you better buy a compass.

Contact Info:
Visitor Center
505-847-2585
www.nps.gov/sapu

Fee: no fees, but donations appreciated; how about building up some good karma by dropping a few greenbacks in the box?

Hours: open daily; summer (Memorial Day–Labor Day) 9 a.m.–6 p.m., winter 9 a.m.–5 p.m.

Best time to visit: anytime except when it's really hot in midsummer

Camping/Lodging: camping in Cibola National Forest, lodging in Mountainair

Access: good paved road to site with easy short paths around ruins; much of this is handicap accessible; the petroglyph hike is a moderate 1 mile round trip

Jon's Rating: ★★★★☆ (archaeology)

Jon's Notes:
When you come around the bend and see Abo Ruins, you have two conflicting thoughts—*What a great place to live!* and *Why did they build this huge mission way out here?* The answer lies in history and the cobwebs of Spanish expansionism in the early 17th century. For whatever reason, and probably owing to the thriving native population, the Franciscan missionaries thought it was a great place to preach the divine word. And when they decided that, the building projects began!

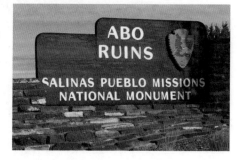

LEFT: Not your run-of-the-mill McMansion-on-the-Prairie.

MORE, BIGGER, AND BETTER...

The Franciscans were no fools—they knew when they had a good thing going and you just couldn't beat free local labor. By the time they completed the first church in the late 1620s, they had already decided it was obsolete. A bigger and better church was required. Alas, the party didn't last. Everyone filed out of the place about the mid 1670s, including the Franciscans, as a result of a never-ending drought.

An artist's conception of Abo, back in the day when the friar had his groove on.

Artwork by Vernon Morris

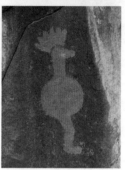

Of the three primary ruins in the Salinas Pueblo Missions National Monument, this site has the best petroglyphs.

DOING PETROS

Of the three ruins which comprise Salinas Pueblo Missions National Monument, this is the only one where you can also see rock art. It's not on the brochure and it's not on any signs nor along the formal paths, so you have to ask. But don't be afraid—the rangers are friendly, knowledgeable and happy to lead you to them. The petroglyphs which abide here are excellent and the walk is easy and scenic.

Directions: From Albuquerque, head west on I-40 to exit 108. From here, drive southwest on Reservation Route 23 about 13 miles to Acoma. The Sky City Cultural Center is on the corner when you connect with Reservation Route 38. It's the nicest building in town.

Contact Info:
Sky City Cultural Center
800-747-0181
http://sccc.acomaskycity.org

Fee: per person tour fees, plus camera fees, all of which help perpetuate the good work here

Hours: tours are offered daily every hour; there are some times when tours are not offered: June 24 & 29, July 10–13, & 25, the first or second weekend in October, and the first Saturday in December; other closures can occur without notice

Best time to visit: we like this place best in the fall, but just about anytime is a good time—except during tribal ceremonies

Camping/Lodging: closest lodging and camping are north of Acoma at the Sky City Casino at I-40

Access: easy access—a shuttle bus takes you to the top and back down again; the tour takes about 1½ hours; call ahead to make sure the mesa is not closed for tribal ceremonies

Jon's Rating: ★★★★☆ (archaeology)
★★★☆☆ (geology)

Jon's Notes:
If you spend any time in New Mexico at all, you'll no doubt hear of Acoma. Built atop a sheer-walled, 370-foot sandstone butte in a broad, picturesque valley southwest of Albuquerque, Sky City has remained suspended in time for over two millennia. It is reputed to be the oldest continuously-inhabited community in North America and is known worldwide for its unique art and rich culture. You can only visit with a guided tour, but these are guaranteed to please even the most jaded "I don't do tours" kind of person. While on the tour ask about the story of Enchanted Mesa that resides nearby. And if you're in half-decent physical shape, be sure to take the ancient stairway down to the bottom, once the only access to the top. Plan to spend some time in the excellent museum afterwards.

LEFT: The main church atop Acoma.

ABOVE: Enchanted Mesa in the distance. Acoma legend tells the story of a group of ancestors who were trapped atop the mesa after a landslide took out the only approach.

RIGHT: A view along the traditional route to the top of Acoma mesa.

SHOPPING ATOP THE MESA

Acoma is known for its distinctive pottery styles. While on the tour you will encounter several of the mesa-top residents who have displays of their art for sale along the tour route. You may wonder—is this the real thing? Well, more or less. If you want the most genuine article and are willing to pay for it, look for pottery that was hand-thrown, fired and painted all by the artist. Don't be afraid to ask. The less-expensive option is production-run figures and pots that are not made locally but are finished and hand-painted here. (Artwork by Vernon Morris)

Traditional living atop Acoma mesa.

Directions: From Bloomfield, head south on US 550 about 15 miles. Turn left (east) on County 7175 (there is a sign). Follow the gravel road into the area. The campground is at the end, about 6 miles from US 550, but there are plenty of places to admire the view or play Scrabble before you get there.

Contact Info:
BLM Farmington Field Office
505-599-8900
www.blm.gov/nm/st/en/prog/recreation/farmington/Angel_Peak.html

Fee: no fees, not even for camping; you can help out by donating to the *Archaeological Conservancy*; contact them at www.americanarchaeology.org

Hours: open daily all year

Best time to visit: when you're in the mood—it's as simple as that; you'll be wondering why you didn't come here sooner

Camping/Lodging: basic camping on-site; nearest improved camping and lodging in Bloomfield

Access: County 7175 can become impassable for regular cars in bad weather; hikes can be of any length and difficulty

Jon's Rating: ★★★★☆ (geology)

Jon's Notes:
It might look like the Badlands of South Dakota and in many ways it's very similar—minus, of course, Wall Drug and the free ice water. Weak, unconsolidated sediments are quickly eroding from the mesas and buttes, exposing the colorful layers along their flanks. You can travel far and wide in this area, but be sure to keep your bearings and take plenty of water, whether you head out on foot or on a camel. And, one other thing, if it has rained recently this is a great place for mud wrestling!

LEFT: In case you hadn't noticed, there's a whole lot of geology going on here.

These beds (top) contain 60-million-year-old fossil mammals, although the hawk (right) is probably looking for something a little more recent.

PAINTING THE TOWN

Here's some nifty geologic trivia for you, certain to spice up that boring bachelor party: Iron is the most common coloring agent on Earth. It's the reason lava is black (actually it's a very dark brown) and rust is, well, rust-colored. The bright-hued exposures here are colored primarily by iron oxides which impart the tans, browns, pinks, and reds to the wild geology already here. Throw in early morning or late afternoon filtered sunlight and the result is a cornucopia of color and texture, a veritable feast for your eyes and your camera.

Most of Angel Peak is made up of various sandstones and clay beds of the Nacimiento Formation, a 60-million-year-old deposit which formed after the dinosaurs called it quits.

AZTEC ARCHES

4

Directions: Anasazi Arch: From Aztec, drive north on US 550 about 11 miles to left on CR 2300 after town of Cedar Hill. In 1.25 miles, take a right onto CR 2310. In 2.5 miles, turn right just after the compressor station. Drive across the arroyo (if passable! if not, park here) and take the left fork at the old Phillips Petroleum sign on the other side. Keep left and park at the clearing at the base of a cliff. The trail leads to the left uphill through some exposed vertical spots. Be careful! **Arch Rock**: From Aztec, drive north on US 550 about 4 miles. Take a right on Hart Canyon Road (CR 2770) and travel 6.1 miles. Take a left up the hill and travel 0.7 miles. Take another left at a fork and drive for about 0.5 miles. Arch Rock will be on the right about 100 yards off the road.

Contact Info:
Aztec Chamber & Visitors Center
505-334-9551
www.aztecnm.com

Fee: no fees; you can help out by visiting the Aztec Museum and Pioneer Village in town at 125 N. Main Ave.; while there make a donation.

Hours: always open, but keep it to daylight hours

Best time to visit: don't try the roads when the weather is bad; fall and summer are best

Camping/Lodging: basic camping on BLM land; improved camping at Navajo Reservoir and lodging in Aztec

Access: some roads may be impassable in bad weather; hiking to and around Arch Rock is easy; the hike to Anasazi Arch is a moderate-to-difficult 1.2 miles (round trip) with some exposed sections

Jon's Rating: ★★★★☆ (geology)
★★☆☆☆ (archaeology)

Jon's Notes:
Obviously the space aliens responsible for creating these geologic phenomena honed their skills here before going public with it all in Arches National Park, Utah. Although not quite as spectacular as their cousins 150 miles northwest, these monuments are a great addition to your visit in the area. Anasazi Arch is especially reminiscent of Delicate Arch in Utah. There are several arches in the area and be sure to check out Simon Canyon Ruin, not far down the road to the east.

LEFT: The arches found around here are smaller and more manageable than those in Utah. Here Anasazi Arch shows off its figure.

ABOVE: Outstanding
in its field—Arch Rock.

RIGHT: Octopus Arch
actually has three arch-
es connected together
in one span. It really
does look something
like an octopus.

TO ARCH OR NOT TO ARCH

The processes by which nature creates a natural arch or bridge can be quite varied. In general, the story starts with formation of a ridge or dike of rock with roughly parallel sides sticking out from the surrounding landform. The height of this feature usually far exceeds its thickness. Erosional forces attack the exposure but make faster work of the weaker sediments below the area of the span. Eventually the lower sides erode completely through, allowing for passage of birds, critters and maybe even flying saucers.

The local wildlife enjoy the arches too. So please respect their rights—do not trample the vegetation, climb the arches, or hassle the animals.

AZTEC RUINS NATIONAL MONUMENT

5

Directions: Aztec Ruins National Monument is very cleverly located on Ruins Road about 0.5 miles north of NM 516, in the City of Aztec. The ancient Aztecs are, no doubt, proud of this place, even though they had no hand in building it.

Contact Info:
Park Headquarters
505-334-6174
www.nps.gov/azru

Fee: per person entrance fee

Hours: open daily; summer (Memorial Day–Labor Day) 8 a.m.–6 p.m., winter 8 a.m.–5 p.m.; closed Thanksgiving, Christmas and New Year's

Best time to visit: go for it whenever you find the time to head to the hills

Camping/Lodging: basic camping on BLM land, improved camping and lodging in Aztec

Access: easy paved trails around ruins, much of this site is accessible for those with disabilities

Jon's Rating: ★★★★☆ (archaeology)

Jon's Notes:
This massive pueblo site has been admirably excavated and preserved and is now yours to enjoy. A huge, full-scale "great kiva" has been constructed on the grounds, modeled after the one found on-site. You are permitted to access many of the ruins, giving you that kid-like feel-ing of playing in "the fort" when you were younger. There's also a great museum at the visitor center. So what I'm trying to say here is: You really have no excuse for not visiting Aztec Ruins—get over and check it out.

LEFT: Remains of a kiva and surrounding rooms. ABOVE: A full-scale reconstruction of a kiva.

The neat thing is you can walk around and through many of the ruins here.

EARLY TIMESHARES

Around 1100 AD the condo biz was booming in Aztec, prompting ancestral Pueblo developers to embark on an ambitious building project on the banks of the Animas River. In less than 30 years, they built a monumental 500-room pueblo standing three-stories high and stretching longer than a football field. Rumor has it the project was so successful that McDonald's inquired about opening a franchise here in 1150 but was denied. Ronald wasn't happy about that.

An artist's rendition of a working kiva.

Artwork by Vernon Morris

BANDELIER NATIONAL MONUMENT

6

Directions: From White Rock, travel southwest on NM 4 about 8.5 miles. The Bandelier Monument entrance is on the left side of the road. We got you to this point, now the rest is up to you . . .

Contact Info:
Visitor Information
505-672-3861
www.nps.gov/band

Fee: vehicle entrance fee

Hours: open daily, but hours vary with season; closed Christmas and New Year's

Best time to visit: anytime except when it's snowed in, might be a tad difficult then

Camping/Lodging: campground in the park; lodging in Los Alamos

Access: easy to very difficult depending on the trail; there are paved trails in parts, steep ladders and ancient, exposed stairways in others

Jon's Rating: ★★★★★ (archaeology)
★★★☆☆ (geology)

Jon's Notes:
When times get tuff, the tough get going! This region is covered with huge deposits of "tuff," a stable but workable volcanic rock which was exploited by the local developers for construction of apartments and condos. (See page 227 for the glossary entry for tuff for more information.) The ancestral Pueblo people who lived here produced an impressive array of pottery and other artifacts beginning more than 10,000 years ago. There are ruins all over the place! Many are easily accessible, and the museum is first-rate. If you're a fan of ancient ruins, you will not want to miss this unique place.

LEFT: It's all about location, they say. But, in this case, it's also all about geology.

Civic planners had a fun time trying to control the sprawl here. All kinds of homes were carved out of the friable tuff.

LOCAL HOUSING MARKET TAKES A DIVE

There's plenty of evidence that people have been frequenting this area for over 10,000 years. The early occupants were nomadic, chasing game wherever they could find it—a thoroughly frustrating experience being as they were without ATVs or high-power rifles. But about 1150 A.D. the tune changed, and the Ancients began building more permanent settlements here. A mega housing boom ensued and it was all pretty rosy for quite a while. By 1550, however, the boom went bust. The occupants effectively abandoned the place, moving to better pueblos along the Rio Grande. Real estate agents at the time could do little else than watch as the local housing market collapsed while their listings went untouched.

Living like Wayne Newton. It was inevitable: The good life of multistory condos could not be denied to the residents of Bandelier.

An example of a "cavate"; not your average linen closet, but it'll work in a pinch.

LONG HOUSE CAVATES AND VIGAS

I'm gonna be a man about this and tell you right up front here I have no clue how or why anyone would create such risible terms: "Cavate" is a combination of the words cave (a hollow passage into the earth) and excavate (to hollow out). Here it refers to a form of architecture used by the Ancients at ruins like Long House where they hollowed out areas in the soft sandstone to use for living and storage. "Viga" is an even more nebulous term which refers to a hand-hewn timber. "Viga holes" are places carved into the cliff walls to hold the ends of those timbers. Such holes show that Long House was once a two to three story structure. (Artwork by Vernon Morris)

WHAT'S A BANDELIER?

The name has nothing to do with bands—neither rock-n-roll, big bands, nor marauding bands of hoodlums from New York City. Instead it refers to the famous anthropologist/archaeologist Adolph Bandelier who made it his life's work to live with, study, and record the Pueblo peoples of the Southwest. In 1880 Bandelier befriended members of the Cochiti Pueblo who offered to show him their ancestral homelands and ultimately brought him to Frijoles Canyon. "Dude, this is totally awesome!" he reportedly said upon seeing the richness of ruins.

The tuff at Bandelier is ideal for carving out large rooms with built-in cabinetry.

BANDERA VOLCANO AND ICE CAVE

7

Directions: Located approximately 28 miles southwest of Grants, off NM 53 at mile marker 61. The entrance drive is about 4 miles west of the El Malpais Information Center.

Contact Info:
General Information
888-ICE-CAVE
www.icecaves.com

Fee: per person entrance fee

Hours: open every day from 8 a.m. to one hour before sunset

Best time to visit: in my humble, yet accurate opinion, fall is the nicest, but you can go anytime it suits you

Camping/Lodging: basic camping on BLM land in El Malpais; improved camping and lodging in Grants

Access: easy maintained gravel trails to volcano and ice cave

Jon's Rating: ★★★☆☆ (geology)

Jon's Notes:
There's not likely to be another chance for you to visit a genuine ice cave so you may as well stop in here while you have a chance, especially if it's a hot day. Here you effectively have two attractions in one—a bona fide ice cave (technically a lava tube) plus a bona fide volcano—one of which is work-ing, the other of which is not (thankfully). Here's how this ice cave works: During the winter months the lava tube traps cold air and the ice-maker goes into full production, accumulating copious amounts of ice. Since this particular tube is fairly deep and thus well insulated even in the heat of summer the place is cold as ice (pun intended). Although there is some melt-

ing in summer, the ice survives until the next winter and the process starts again. Ice persists year-round and an "ice cave" is the result. And if that isn't cool enough for you, the area is picturesque, the hikes are easy, and the people are friendly, so why not?

LEFT: Inside the belly of the beast, the annual accumulation sometimes turns green due to microbes in the ice.

ABOVE: Porous basalt has great insulation capabilities. Add a little water supply, some cold winters, and presto! you've got yourself an ice cave.

RIGHT: Bandera volcano is a nice little caldera reachable via an easy hike from the visitor center.

CHILLING OUT

Not surprisingly, the ice here has been famous for thousands of years. It was utilized by all manner of early entrepreneurs in the refrigeration business, from the ancient traders plying the Zuni-Acoma Trail to white pioneers looking for something to cool down their sarsaparilla root beer. Later, as demand grew to maintain area ice boxes, the crystalline H_2O was actually mined from the hole and sold locally. But then, in the early 1900s, Dr. Willis Carrier invented refrigeration and effectively ruined the whole party.

Unlike other ice caves which are remote and difficult to access, this one has an easy walkway right to the main ice flow.

BISTI/DE-NA-ZIN WILDERNESS

8

Directions: From Farmington, head south on NM 371 about 36.5 miles. Turn left on County Road 7297 and follow the gravel road for approximately 2 miles to the Bisti parking lot. The hoodoos are about 0.75 miles one-way from this lot and you can see the area from the car.

Contact Info:
Farmington Field Office
505-564-7600
www.blm.gov/nm/bisti

Fee: no fees, but here's how you can help—make a donation to New Mexico SiteWatch program via the Archaeological Society of New Mexico (www.newmexico-archaeology.org); be sure to label the check "For SiteWatch"

Hours: always open, but be sure to visit during daytime

Best time to visit: avoid bad weather and midsummer heat

Camping/Lodging: basic camping here on BLM land; closest lodging is Farmington

Access: easy to very difficult terrain in park with few real trails; be careful, pay attention to your route, and take plenty of water

Jon's Rating: ★★★½ (geology)

Jon's Notes:
The Cretaceous age (about 65 million years ago) Fruitland Formation makes up most of what you'll see while in these badlands. It's made up of interbedded sandstone, shale, mudstone, coal, and silt. The weathering of the sandstone forms the many spires and hoodoos found throughout the area, just like those in the Ojito Wilderness (pg. 151) and places like it. There's plenty of room to wonder and wander among the strange geologic worlds. Just don't get lost! There are few recognizable trails here and most of them peter out in the vacant wilds. It's easy to get distracted, but remember how to get back to the car.

LEFT: There's no accounting for some people's choice of head gear.

The rocks of the Fruitland Formation (above) do a good job of preserving and petrifying the old trees (right) which grew nearby here in the Cretaceous, about 65 million years ago.

HOODOO?

Do what? Some words are just plain inexplicable. Most geologic terms have their origins in Europe or the British Isles, where geology got its mojo going. But "hoodoo?" What's up with that? Sorry, I can't help you on the origin here. In geology slang, the term refers to weird erosional rock formations. Most of the time these are strange sci-fi shaped pillars of rock, bent and gnarled by erosion and often capped by a large slab of harder rock, which protects the softer rock beneath.

The term "Bisti" is considered a Navajo word for badlands. The local lizards don't care what it means, so long as you Leave No Trace (see glossary for info on this method of travel).

Directions: Located in Santa Rosa. From I-40 exit #275, head south on Historic Route 66/US 84 about 0.3 miles to left on Lake Drive. In 0.2 miles, turn left onto S. 9th St. Follow this for 0.5 miles to left turn to the parking area. NOTE: Blue Hole is NOT at Lake Park, it's past it.

Contact Info:
Santa Rosa Visitor Information
575-472-3404
www.santarosanm.org

Fee: no fee to visit and take a swim, but you need a permit to SCUBA dive

Hours: open daily, but the dive center is only regularly open in the summer or by appointment

Best time to visit: if you're cruising down the interstate in the summer it's a great place to cool off

Camping/Lodging: camping and lodging in town nearby

Access: step out of your car, walk 20 steps to the edge and jump in!

Jon's Rating: ★★★☆☆ (geology)

Jon's Notes:
Although it may seem out of place in the middle of the desert, Blue Hole is actually quite at home here, geologically speaking. The town of Santa Rosa sits in a giant karst (see the glossary) depression caused by water solutions dissolving subsurface rocks of the San Andres Formation, a limestone which formed in shallow seas about 250 million years ago. When the dissolution action nears the surface, the overlying rocks sometimes collapse, forming your typical sinkhole. Of these, Blue Hole is the most famous and accessible. It's a cool, fish-bowl-like experience if you take the plunge and/or SCUBA dive here. In the blistering heat of summer, it's an especially welcoming dip that feels like Nirvana.

But don't get Blue Hole proper confused with the family lake/park nearby. You'll know you're in the right place when you see it.

LEFT: It's big, it's deep and it's blue. In the summer it's a refreshing place to cool off, too.

BOTTOMLESS LAKES STATE PARK

Directions: From Roswell, head east on US 380 for 12 miles and then south on NM 409 for 3 miles. Keep your eyes on the road—we don't want you driving over the edge into the bottomless abyss.

Contact Info:
Park Info
575-624-6058
www.emnrd.state.nm.us/PRD/bottomless.htm

Fee: vehicle entrance fee

Hours: always open, but best in the daytime; Lea Lake day use area open 7 a.m.–9 p.m. daily

Best time to visit: especially nice in the summer and fall but you can visit anytime

Camping/Lodging: improved camping on-site; lodging in Roswell

Access: easy to moderate hiking around formations, but no swimming except at Lea Lake

Jon's Rating: ★★★★☆ (geology)

Jon's Notes:
It's no wonder the people of Roswell are convinced space aliens have invaded their town. Judging by the reports in Weekly World News and other credible sources, there's ample evidence the mothership launched plenty of flying saucers around here. And when you see Bottomless Lakes State Park, you'll see why—it's a great place to land! Eight gigantic sink-holes have collected along this stretch of the Pecos River and many are full of spring water and support sizeable lakes. The largest—Lea Lake —has a nice campground and groomed beach making it *the* place to be in the summertime heat, whether you're from planet Earth or elsewhere.

LEFT: It looks man-made, but it's better than that. One of several cenotes in this park near Roswell.

A great place to swim in the summer—Lea Lake, the largest lake in the park.

COOL GEOLOGY

Bottomless Lakes State Park has an interesting geology that is uniquely its own. The park is situated along an escarpment of Permian age (230 million years ago) rock from the Artesia Group that was tilted up, effectively blocking the flow of groundwater flowing from the Sacramento Mountains. Once trapped, the water slowly dissolved the limestone that comprises a good portion of the sediments, forming caves and caverns. Later, the roofs of some of these cavities collapsed, resulting in spring pools called *cenotes*. It's a rather hip term employed mostly by cool geologists in the know, but you'll be allowed to incorporate it in your own upper-class lexicon once you've visited the area and seen it for yourself.

THROW MONEY

Because of the unique nature of this environment, some rare and endangered species are found at Bottomless Lakes. The small Pecos Pupfish and the Rainwater Killifish reside in the clean aqua waters here. The Eastern Barking Frog and the Cricket Frog, also endangered species, live in the park as well. So please help these cool critters out by not throwing anything, including coins, into the water or on land. If you want to throw money, wait until the rangers show up and throw it at them. They'll use it to help keep the place healthy.

The tower and main visitor complex at Lea Lake.

CAPULIN VOLCANO NATIONAL MONUMENT

Directions: The park entrance is on New Mexico Highway 325, 3 miles north of the town of Capulin, which hopefully hasn't been destroyed by an eruption before you get there. If it has, stay calm and proceed to shop like nothing ever happened.

Contact Info:
Visitor Center
575-278-2201
www.nps.gov/cavo

Fee: vehicle entrance fee

Hours: the park is open daily except New Year's, Thanksgiving, and Christmas

Best time to visit: whenever the road is not snowed in is a fine time to visit; even in the hot summer there's generally a nice breeze up here

Camping/Lodging: improved camping in Capulin, outside of the park; the closest lodging is in Raton

Access: you drive right up to the top where a moderate 1-mile round-trip paved path circles the rim

Jon's Rating: ★★★★☆ (geology)

Jon's Notes:
Capulin Volcano is probably the best example of a symmetrical cinder cone in the entire region. It's not too old, either—about 60,000 years, last time we checked. There are educational stations posted regularly along the trails that follow around the rim. The cone is about a mile in diameter and 400 feet deep. Do your own math—it's a big hole! Even better, it's one of the most accessible volcanoes too—you can drive right up it almost to the top. It has a fantastic view, even from the parking lot.

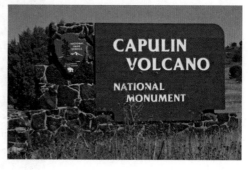

LEFT: The view from the top of Capulin shows other cinder cones in the distance.

Two views from the trail: the inside of the caldera (top), and along the rim (bottom).

LIFE OF THE PARTY

Police records show that approximately 60,000 years ago things around here got a little testy. It really wouldn't have been so bad except the fact that the local volcano had a tizzy-fit, spewing off at the mouth and peeving all the neighbors by building a cinder cone more than 1,000 feet high right outside town. Eventually, however, everything returned to normal—all happy-happy, as it were—and Capulin Volcano has kept his big mouth shut ever since. Let's hope he stays that way!

Thar she blows! Capulin has a volcanic fit 60,000 years ago.

Artwork by Vernon Morris

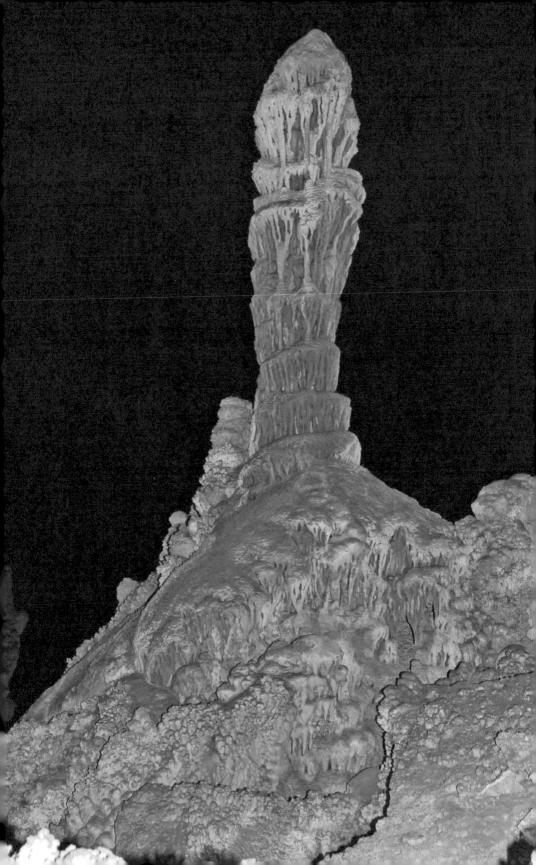

CARLSBAD CAVERNS NATIONAL PARK

Directions: From Carlsbad, follow US 180/62 approximately 20 miles southwest to White's City where you turn right (west) on NM 7. The visitor center and cavern entrance are about 7 miles away.

Contact Info:
Park Information
575-785-2232
www.nps.gov/cave

Fee: per person entrance fee, but those 15 and under are free

Hours: open daily; summer (Memorial Day–Labor Day) 8 a.m.–7 p.m., winter 8 a.m.–5 p.m., but closed Christmas; last entrance to the underground is usually 2 hours before closing, but the last entry through the natural entry is 3 to 3 1/2 hours before closing

Best time to visit: absolutely anytime you can get here is a great time to get down underground; give yourself plenty of time

Camping/Lodging: improved camping and lodging in White's City

Access: nice and easy paved paths through most of the tour areas; there's even a snack bar down under!

Jon's Rating: ★★★★★ (geology)

Jon's Notes:
If you haven't been here, you've not experienced the crowning glory of America's underground. Carlsbad Caverns National Park is home to some of the most impressive and renowned caves in the world. The main cavern—Carlsbad—is one of the greatest subterranean experiences anywhere. And then there's the Mecca of the underworld—Lechuguilla—which, for scientific reasons, is off-limits to the general public. There are many others here as well. The setting for all this is quite beautiful—tucked away in a remote area of the Chihuahuan Desert and Guadalupe Mountains where you'd never suspect the colossal cavities that lie beneath the surface.

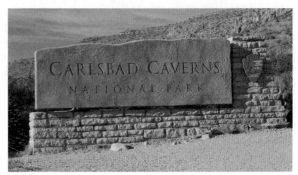

LEFT: The best of the underworld can be seen at Carlsbad Caverns.

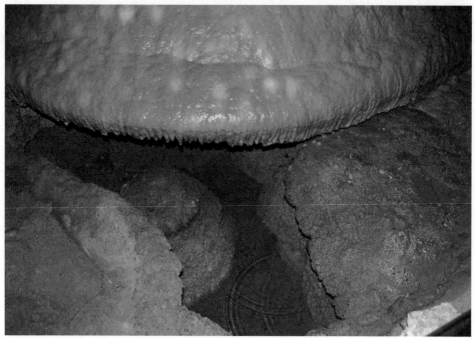

A rimstone dam attests that the formations here are still active.

GET DOWN UNDERGROUND

There are literally hundreds of distinct caves inside Carlsbad Caverns National Park. Thankfully, the Park Service allows you access to several subterranean adventures. You can pick from a variety of experiences and levels of difficulty. These ranger-led tours are for the more adventurous who don't mind getting dirty (most of the fun of caving is getting covered in mud!) You will need some of your own equipment (the park provides headgear) and a change of clothes. Some of these cavities—Kings Palace, Hall of the White Giant, Left Hand Tunnel—are in Carlsbad itself. Others—Slaughter Canyon Cave and Spider Cave among them—are their own unique adventures not associated with the main cave. Check the website or the visitor center. Advance reservations are highly recommended.

HOW BIG IS BIG?

You won't need to feed money into this wow-o-meter because it will be maxed out already. The term "Big Room" is a woefully inadequate understatement for the largest cavern in the park and the largest in the USA. At 8.2 acres, it's large enough to house several Super Wal-Marts but, thankfully, it isn't crowded with anything except 100% natural goods. The place is crammed wall-to-wall with active cave formations—from tiny soda-straws and helictites to huge stalactites, stalagmites, and columns—all in a rainbow of colors. The best part is, this is a "self-guided" tour where you can set your own pace and dawdle as long as you wish. Every turn is another "wow."

Gigantic stalagmites in the "Big Room."

LECHUGUILLA CAVE

Wanna mine crap for a living? No? Well, someone has to do it! Until 1986, Lechuguilla was known mostly as a source of bat guano (which is used in the manufacture of gunpowder and fertilizer, believe it or not). The guano actually proved to be too old to use for fertilizer, but miners happened to hear wind whistling up through cracks in the rocks of the floor. This, of course, indicated a major cave lay below them. Eventually a group of curious Colorado cavers gained permission from the National Park Service and began digging, searching for more passageways. The breakthrough occurred on May 26, 1986 and the new discovery has since become more than spectacular, with more than 120 miles of passages mapped and a depth so far of 1,604 feet. Lechuguilla has since become known as one of the longest, most spectacular caves in the world. It is especially famous for its gypsum formations.

One of the greatest discoveries in the underworld of North America— Lechuguilla Cave

It's not just the size and abundance of the formations here; it's also the array of colors. A golden stalagmite (left) and orange drapery.

DOING ACID

Typical caves form because of the erosive action of carbonic acid, but that's not the case here. Both Carlsbad and Lechuguilla formed as a result of sulfuric acid dissolution of the regional limestone—a unique process that makes for spectacular results in terms of cave chamber mega-expansion, which creates enough room for giant formations and massive amounts of ornamentation to grow. The sulfuric acid is believed to be a result of hydrogen sulfide solutions released from oil reservoirs far below, which mix with groundwater percolating through the cracks and crevices of the rock above. Because the concentration of sulfuric acid is far greater than would normally occur in nature, the limestone was aggressively attacked and chemically eroded much faster than in other caverns.

Directions: From Grants, take I-40 west to exit 63 at Prewitt. Connect with Historic Route 66 on the north side of I-40. Turn right on Rt. 66 and travel east about 0.5 miles toward Prewitt, then turn left onto County 19 and drive past the turn-off for Escalante Generating Station. Follow 19 north for 4.2 miles. Park in the small pullout next to the road on the left side.

Contact Info:
BLM Rio Puerco Resource Area
505-761-8700
http://en.wikipedia.org/wiki/Casamero_Pueblo,_New_Mexico

Fee: no fees, but since you're such a nice person and want to do your share to help out, make a donation to the Archaeological Conservancy; contact them at www.americanarchaeology.org

Hours: always open—but best in the daytime

Best time to visit: it's easy to stop here anytime

Camping/Lodging: improved camping and lodging in Grants

Access: the trail to this site is easy; it's not paved, but it is easy

Jon's Rating: ★★★★★ (archaeology)

Jon's Notes:
Casamero Pueblo could be called an orphan child of Chaco Canyon. Although it was affiliated with the great cultural center to the north, it's not the sort of place that gives you any concept of the magnitude or diversity for which Chaco is known. Still it is an interesting place to stop at, especially if you are on your way to Chaco Canyon proper. When you get into your car again and make the long drive to the main complex, you'll have some appreciation for the vastness of the Chaco Culture, which influenced even far-flung places like Casamero. Although tiny by comparison, the folks who lived here had a great view, and as they say in real estate, it's all about location, location, location!

LEFT: A room with a view.

Directions: The area is approximately 5 miles NE of Glenwood, NM, at the end of NM Hwy 174 a.k.a. Catwalk Road.

Contact Info:
Gila National Forest
Glenwood Ranger Station
505-539-2722
www.fs.usda.gov/recmain/gila/recreation

Fee: there is a modest vehicle entrance fee, but on the first day of each month it's free!

Hours: the Catwalk is a day-use area only, and is open daily

Best time to visit: anytime, except during a 100-year flood (I'm serious about that!)

Camping/Lodging: camping is available at nearby Gila National Forest; please note there is NO camping at the Catwalk itself; lodging is available in Glenwood or Silver City

Access: the roads are good and the catwalk even better; with your choice of easy or moderate trails

Jon's Rating: ★★★★☆ (geology)

Jon's Notes:
The "Catwalk" was originally built atop a water pipeline that ran through the slot of Whitewater Canyon sometime in the early part of the 20th century. It supplied water and power to a nearby mill. In 1935, the Civilian Conservation Corps built the first official walkway atop the piping so visitors could explore and enjoy the canyon. Since then, the Forest Service has done an admirable job of expanding on this theme. There are several spots where visitors can leave the causeway and relax on the banks of the stream, and even one where you can swim in a perfect pool with a small waterfall on one end. Whitewater Picnic Area lies at the entrance to the catwalk and offers opportunities for a nice, quiet picnic under the Sycamores. It's an incredible place.

LEFT: One way to make the most of a huge plumbing job.

THE LAND OF CHOICES

In most places when you're hiking you don't often get choices of difficulty, but you do here. Usually there's one path and that's that. But guess what—this is America and we can have fries with that order if we want to! The original trail follows a footpath along the north side of the canyon, accessing the catwalk and extending beyond it for a 2.2-mile round trip excursion of moderate difficulty. On the south side, the Forest Service has installed a "universal trail" (mostly paved), which is fully handicap-accessible that runs for approximately 0.6 miles (one-way). It ends at the first set of stairs.

What a great place to swim!

Views along the upper part of the scenic trail

BLOWING BUBBLES

As you enter the canyon proper you'll notice the chocolate brown walls are perforated with cavities, each lined with tiny crystals. Thirty-five million years ago, more or less, this area was a hotbed of volcanic activity. But instead of one giant boisterous volcano, there were several smaller vents that puffed and fumed and spewed lava, ash, and debris all over the place until it was hundreds of feet thick. Some of the resulting rock trapped steam bubbles as it cooled. These became the initial cavities you see here. Later, as groundwater solutions percolated through them, they became lined with crystals, forming *geodes*.

Directions: From Bloomfield, head south on US 550 about 48 miles. At mile 112.5 (3 miles southeast of Nageezi) turn right on County 7900. The route is clearly signed from US 550 to the park boundary (21 miles). The drive includes 8 miles of paved road (CR 7900) and 13 miles of rough dirt road (CR 7950). There is a route from the south but it becomes impassable at times, so call ahead if you intend to drive from that direction.

Contact Info:
Visitor Information
505-786-7014 x221
www.nps.gov/chcu

Fee: vehicle entrance fee

Hours: the park is always open; the visitor center is open 8 a.m.–5 p.m. daily but closed Thanksgiving, Christmas, and New Year's

Best time to visit: April–May and September–October are the best times to visit Chaco

Camping/Lodging: limited basic camping on-site, other basic camping on BLM land to the northeast; improved camping and lodging in Bloomfield

Access: the roads in are rough but thankfully not too long; hiking is easy–difficult depending on the place

Jon's Rating: ★★★★★ (archaeology)

Jon's Notes:
There's no getting around the washboard roads on the way to Chaco. But the fact remains—it is well worth the hassle and all the more impressive as a result. Chaco Culture is the premier archaeological site in New Mexico and one of the finest in the world. There are hundreds of sites within the park, many of which are open for you to explore. Six major sites are located along the 9-mile long Canyon Loop Drive. The problem is finding the time to do it all. Don't worry—you won't, so you'll just have to come back. Just don't count on the access roads getting any better.

LEFT: One of the grandest building complexes of ancient times is now one of the greatest treasures of the modern world.

The "Chacoan Event" was one of the most impressive building campaigns to ever occur in North America.

DONALD TRUMP WOULD HAVE LOVED IT

You never saw such an enterprise. Even to this day Chaco Canyon and the Chaco Culture represent one of the greatest development projects ever in North America. To say it was a major force in Pre-Columbian cultural influence is a gross understatement. From about 850 to 1150 AD (that's 300 years, in case you're wondering)—the peak of the "Chacoan event"—over a dozen huge complexes of buildings were erected, many of which would dwarf the average urban shopping mall. Even though the exodus was pretty much complete by the mid 1200s, the structures at Chaco Canyon remained the largest buildings in North America until the 19th century. The sites are still considered sacred to several Native American tribes that continue to frequent the area.

Kivas were a big thing back in the day. Since Chaco had a big population they built some HUGE ones here.

*Several kivas and
multilevel buildings
are evident in all the
major pueblos of
Chaco canyon.*

MOVING ON

As in other ancient ruins of the southwest, climate change is thought to have had a major impact on the livelihood of the inhabitants of Chaco Canyon. A 50-year drought, which started about 1130, likely led to the departure of Chacoans and the eventual abandonment of the canyon. By 1150 the whole place was pretty much deserted and, as a result, the out-of-town developers nixed their bold plans to build an amusement park and 18-hole golf course here.

Two studies in civic pride: Architecture (left) and art.

The museum here shows off zillions of artifacts, some of which were properly collected by scientists with a permit (right), and some of which were not (above).

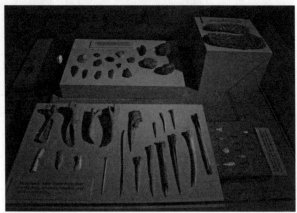

CHACO FLY-BY

Scientific research has been an integral part of Chaco Canyon since before it became a park in 1907. The first aerial photographs of Chaco Canyon were taken from Charles Lindbergh's airplane by his wife Anne Morrow Lindbergh in 1929. The museum collection contains approximately one million artifacts from over 120 sites in Chaco Canyon and the surrounding region. Because most of the artifacts were systematically collected and documented, the collections are extremely valuable for scientific studies and are considered some of the finest in the world. (Artwork by Vernon Morris)

One of the educational dioramas in the museum.

CITY OF ROCKS STATE PARK

Directions: From Deming, take US 180 northwest 24 miles, and then go northeast on NM 61 for 4 miles to the park access road. Watch for space aliens—they're all over this place.

Contact Info:
Park Manager
575-536-2800
www.emnrd.state.nm.us/PRD/cityrocks.htm

Fee: vehicle entrance fee

Hours: open daily 7 a.m.–9 p.m.

Best time to visit: anytime, but especially in the fall and winter when it's not so hot

Camping/Lodging: improved camping on-site; lodging in Silver City

Access: easy access—right from your sleeping bag

Jon's Rating: ★★★✬☆ (geology)

Jon's Notes:
There's a place out beyond the foothills of the Gila Mountains which looks like someone got carried away with the playdough. Giant, weird formations pop up out of the plains like some sort of landscape from a science fiction film. But it's all fun because this is nothing less than a giant playground with twist-ed, tilted rocks and winding passages among them. The best part is you can camp right there among the monoliths and play all night long if you want to. Just keep your eye peeled for little green men.

LEFT: Weird rocks? You bet! And lots of them.

Camping here is great—the sites are right in the middle of the action.

PARTY ON

Most of City of Rocks is a result of a raucous volcanic party that was going on about 30 million years ago outside Silver City. While partying down to Kool and the Gang, some superheated ash got so blitzed that it completely welded itself together. Well, you can imagine what the neighborhood thought about that stunt. Later, as the immature brat was growing up, fractures riddled the rock and exposed it to some serious weathering discipline. The cracks widened as the gremlins of wind and rain heaped on all manner of physical insult, eventually leaving the punished remains we see today.

I understand people like to name things—but really now, "Toilet Seat Rock?" (left) What's up with that idea? "Who cares!" exclaims a local leaf-footed bug (right).

CLAYTON LAKE STATE PARK

Directions: Clayton Lake State Park is 12 miles north of Clayton on NM 370. Keep an eye peeled for dinosaurs—they've been known to party-down around here.

Contact Info:
Park Information
575-374-8808
www.emnrd.state.nm.us/PRD/Clayton.htm

Fee: vehicle entrance fee

Hours: open daily 6 a.m.–9 p.m.

Best time to visit: especially nice in the spring and fall; summer is a good time too with the lake open

Camping/Lodging: improved camping on-site; lodging in Clayton

Access: easy boardwalk around dino stomping area; moderate hiking around rock formations

Jon's Rating: ★★★★☆ (paleontology)
★★★☆☆ (geology)

Jon's Notes:
A hundred million years ago there was an infamous party here at Clayton Lake, one which has gone down in Union County history. The funny thing is, no one would have been the wiser if tell-tale evidence hadn't been accidentally brought to light by a 1982 flood. Torrential rains swelled Clayton Lake to overflowing and washed over and around the earthen dam, scouring away sediment at the same time. When the waters receded, the townsfolk were aghast at what they saw: hundreds of footprints left by dinosaurian party-goers which had reveled in the mud-choked dance floor of the Mesozoic. The whole incident remains hush-hush to this day.

LEFT: Doing the Stomp, way back in the day when it was fashionable.

*Hundreds of dinosaur
tracks were revealed
by The Great Flood—
of 1982.*

THE DINOSAUR FREEWAY

The rocks found at Clayton Lake are Dakota Group sediments which formed along the shore of the Western Interior Seaway, a shallow ocean-ic strait that connected the Gulf of Mexico with the Arctic Ocean during the Cretaceous (100 million years ago). As can be expected, inhabitants from far and wide traveled along the shore of this inland sea, no doubt in search of the perfect seaside resort. So many dinosaur track sites have been found along this stretch that it's been dubbed the "Dinosaur Freeway," a pretty sloppy interpretation, if you ask me, considering that the roads back then weren't even paved. Many of the tracks appear to have been made by Iguanodon-like dinosaurs; large, bipedal herbivores known for their strange thumb-spikes which nevertheless enjoyed sipping their mochas on the beach after sunrise yoga class.

Dinos doing their thing a very long time ago.

Artwork by Vernon Morris

Cool geology and exotic wildlife make for some fun hikes in this area.

There's more than just dino tracks here—there's also a great lake with all the amenities.

CORONADO STATE MONUMENT

18

Directions: Coronado State Monument is north of Albuquerque on State Highway 550/44. From I-25 exit #242, head 1.7 miles west to Kuaua Road and follow it to the visitor center.

Contact Info:
New Mexico Department of Cultural Affairs
505-867-5351
www.nmmonuments.org

Fee: per person entrance fee, but note that there is a combination ticket good for admission to both Jemez and Coronado State Monuments for a couple bucks more

Hours: open Wednesday–Monday, 8:30 a.m.–5 p.m.; closed Tuesdays

Best time to visit: anytime except midsummer; it's just too hot!

Camping/Lodging: improved camping on-site; lodging nearby

Access: easy paved trails around ruins; much is handicap accessible

Jon's Rating: ★★☆☆☆ (archaeology)

Jon's Notes:
This site is named for Francisco Vázquez de Coronado who, by various accounts, was reputed to have camped near here in 1540 on his famous drive into the heart of North America. Coronado was your typical Spanish conquistador—from 1540–1542, he led an expedition in search of gold and the fabled city of Cibola. He trekked through Arizona, New Mexico and other states before finally understanding that Native Americans had little use for, and could hardly care less about, gold. He eventually turned back somewhere in central Kansas. Even today, Kansas is considered a good place to turn around and head home.

LEFT: There are ruins, yes, but they're not from Coronado. They're from local Indians.

This area of riverfront was once a site inhabited by local Indians.

GOING FOR THE GOLD

There was a time when being a conquistador was *de rigueur* for Spanish gentlemen of the day. But you know, sometimes it wasn't all that conquistador-ing is cracked up to be. Take for instance, Coronado: he ran into bad company in the form of friar Marcos de Niza who told him about a fabulous golden city called Cibola way up north. Coronado took the dubious friar at his word and hatched a plan to mount an expedition. The aim, of course, was to empty Cibola of its wealth and return both a hero and rich as a king. Coronado teamed up with some pals and they funded the expedition on their own. But after three disastrous years, he returned to Mexico physically exhausted and financially bankrupt with little interest in the conquistador thing after that.

(Artwork by Vernon Morris)

The small museum has many artifacts from the area, including some excellent pottery.

ECHO AMPHITHEATER

19

Directions: From Espanola, drive 47 miles north on Highway 84. Located on the west side of the road, right off of Highway 84. (From Ghost Ranch entrance, it's approximately 5 miles north.)

Contact Info:
Carson National Forest
575-758-6200
www.fs.fed.us/r3/carson/recreation/trails/trail-descriptions/trail_echo_canyon.shtml

Fee: per vehicle day-use fee

Hours: open daily during daytime hours

Best time to visit: anytime, even in the rain

Camping/Lodging: no camping in Echo Canyon; improved camping on forest nearby; lodging at Ghost Ranch or Espanola

Access: easy ½ mile paved trail to the focal point at Big Echo so you can save your energy for shouting

Jon's Rating: ★★★☆☆ (geology)

Jon's Notes:
In the course of a given week, many people will talk to you, some of whom will tell you stuff you don't want to hear. And then there are the various communication-age electronics which do an admirable job of talking trash to everyone. But, let's face it, there are not many geologic sites that talk back to you as clearly as the Echo Amphitheater. Go ahead, yell your butt off; the rocks don't care. And neither do I, except no obscenities, please.

LEFT: This is one place where you're expected to talk to yourself. So go ahead, start an argument.

Directions: El Malpais is located south of Grants. Two major state highways—NM 53 and NM 117—border the monument. The most convenient place to check in is at the Northwest NM Visitor Center at I-40 exit #85 just east of Grants. There is also another visitor center 24 miles south of Grants on NM 53.

Contact Info:
El Malpais Information Center: 505-783-4774
Northwest New Mexico Visitor Center: 505-876-2783
BLM Ranger Station: 505-280-2918

Fee: no fees, but donations are appreciated; how about building up some good Karma by donating a few greenbacks at one of the visitor centers?

Hours: always open, but visitor center hours vary with season; visit in the daytime—you don't want to get lost here, especially after the sun sets!

Best time to visit: fall and spring; don't hike out here in the middle of summer—you'll roast like a wiener on the barbie

Camping/Lodging: basic camping on BLM land adjacent to the monument; there's a nice campground on NM 117 just south of the ranger station near mile marker 45; improved camping and lodging in Grants

Access: trails run from easy to extreme; in several places, such as Big Tubes Area and Lava Falls, the terrain is so rough that the trails are marked only with cairns; use extreme caution to be sure not to lose the trail; this land is exceptionally harsh! Some of the less-visited lava tubes require permits. Check with the ranger station in advance.

Jon's Rating: ★★★★☆ (geology)
★★☆☆☆ (archaeology)

Jon's Notes:
The term *El Malpais* translates from Spanish to "the badlands," a name which can mean what it says in a harsh way. Most of the area is rough and rugged lava lands which look for all the world like you're walking on the moon. If you decide to explore some of the remote places in the monument, be sure you are prepared with appropriate gear (a GPS is advised), and plenty of water (there are virtually no places to find it out here). One more thing, do not go alone lest you discover the dark side of the name. Believe me, you do not want to get lost in this place.

LEFT: They don't call it Malpais for nothing—it really is a pretty tough landscape.

This famous arch is visible even from the road. Nice of them to think of us before they built it.

THE GOLDEN ARCH

La Ventana Natural Arch is one of the largest arches in New Mexico and one which can give the "Golden Arches" a run for their money. La Ventana is a relic of erosion and weathering of Middle Jurassic Zuni Sandstone which was deposited originally as large, wind-blown sand dunes. These sands were part of a huge dune field that covered much of the four corners area 160 million years ago. It's been said that McDonald's officials were not at all happy about being left out of the swinging party at that time. But things have changed and they now have a few franchises up in Grants.

THE GREAT OOZE

Basalts, cinder cones, and complex lava tubes dominate this landscape which formed mostly as a result of consecutive lava flows pouring onto the surface over a period of about 112,000 years, give-or-take a few centuries. The youngest lava in the park—McCarty's Lava Flow—is dated between 2,000–3,000 years old, while the oldest—El Calderon Lava Flow—is estimated to be 115,000 years old. These were not explosive events, but were more like when a big bucket of thick, dark paint tips over on your mom's floor and oozes out all over her new Persian rug. You'll have to take my word for it, because you definitely don't want to try this experiment at home.

Although it may look barren, lava fields support an entire ecosystem.

Bordering the lava flows are sandstone escarpments with light colors that contrast nicely with the dark basalts below. They afford great views of the park.

DON'T TRY THIS!

While visiting El Malpais in 2007, I met a master cyclist named Doug who had gotten lost in the lava fields and nearly died trying to get out. It started innocently enough, just biking along a nice secluded route off the main road. (Doug is no slouch biker—he logs thousands of miles every year on his bike.) But before he knew it, as the sun began setting, the path disappeared and he was suddenly lost in the middle of a moonscape. He spent the night, confident that he could find the road in the daylight. The next day, the tires blew and he was forced to push/carry his bike over and around the jagged, biting, lava chunks. Then his water ran out. He quickly became dehydrated and delirious. After falling several times, he finally abandoned the bike and stumbled on without it. He spent the second night without water and by morning things were getting very serious. "I nearly gave up," he said, "I prayed a lot." Thankfully, later that day, Doug made it out to the road and back to civilization, lucky to be alive.

There are dozens, perhaps even hundreds, of lava tubes in the park. Many can be visited without a guide, but be sure to call ahead to make sure a permit isn't required. But be sure to go in groups and use caution.

Directions: From Grants at I-40 exit 81, go south on Highway 53 for 42 miles to El Morro National Monument.

Contact Info:
Visitor Center
505-783-4226
www.nps.gov/elmo

Fee: per person entrance fee

Hours: open daily; summer (Memorial Day–Labor Day) 8 a.m.–7 p.m., winter 9 a.m.–5 p.m.; closed Christmas; last access to the trail is about 1 hour before closing

Best time to visit: anytime the weather is good; if there's ice or snow they close the path to the top, although you can still see the inscriptions around the bottom

Camping/Lodging: basic camping on-site; improved camping nearby; lodging in Grants

Access: paved trail along base, moderately difficult trail over top to ruins

Jon's Rating: ★★★★★ (archaeology)
★★★★★ (geology)

Jon's Notes:
Everyone needs a drink now and then and the nice thing about El Morro is its reliable waterhole. Hidden in a notch at the base of this sandstone butte is a small pond that has inspired countless parades of people to stop and party here on their way to someplace else. Even now, it still attracts wildlife year-round. El Morro is a buttress of Zuni Sandstone, about 160 million years old, which was originally deposited as wind-blown sand. As you head up to the top, however, you'll notice a distinct white sandstone cap. This material is Dakota Group sandstone, which, as usual, arrived late for the party—like 100 million years—before settling in for a long nap. But things worked out all right—we now have a pretty cool combination of rocks which make up this monolith, making it even more fun to hike around.

LEFT: View from the top, where the pueblo ruins are located.

It's an imposing structure with a nice view from the top.

PUEBLO WITH A VIEW

Ancestral Puebloans settled on the mesa top over 700 years ago in a series of buildings that may have had as many as 875 rooms. Although we cannot be sure of the date, Native cultures started the tradition of carving images and symbols into El Morro with the pecking of petroglyphs at its base. Later, Spanish and American pioneer travelers stopped here and carved their own inscriptions into the soft sandstone. Today, El Morro protects over 2,000 inscriptions and petroglyphs.

There are over 2000 inscriptions spanning perhaps thousands of years on this one rock.

Directions: Petroglyph Trail: From Ruidoso, drive north on NM 48 for 7 miles. Take a right and head east on NM 220 for 7.3 miles. Before the Sierra Blanca airport turn left onto a dirt road with a BLM sign "Upper Rio Bonito." Without 4WD you are now approaching the point of no return: proceed no farther if you're just in a regular car or RV! From the turn, follow the road downhill 1.7 miles to the "T." Turn right and then left at the first opportunity. This will end at a turn-around near the creek. Follow the footpath to the right and you'll come to Petroglyph Rock in a few hundred yards. **Caves**: You must get a permit in advance from the BLM (call or email) and they'll tell you where to meet.

Contact Info:
BLM Roswell Field Office
575-354-0341
www.blm.gov/nm/fortstanton

Fee: no fees

Hours: open daily during daytime hours; there is no visitor center

Best time to visit: best time is in the summer—but not in the rain!

Camping/Lodging: basic camping on BLM land; improved camping and lodging in Ruidoso

Access: the road to the Petroglyph Trail is hell-to-pay and shouldn't be attempted in vehicles without 4WD; the hike itself is easy; if you're going underground, be aware it can vary from difficult to extreme.

Jon's Rating: ★★★☆☆ (geology)
★☆☆☆☆ (archaeology)

Jon's Notes:
Years ago, someone in the BLM got pretty excited about the rock art possibilities of the Upper Rio Bonito and drafted bold plans for the "National Petroglyph Hiking Trail." If it were up to me, I'd pick a more appropriate location for a "National Petroglyph Hiking Trail." Here's an idea: how about a place that actually has more than one rock with petroglyphs on it! There are some fantastic caves here and you may enjoy them, but only with a permit and guide. Call the BLM Roswell Field Office at 505-627-0272 for more info.

LEFT: Here it is—the climax of the National Petroglyph Hiking Trail, hurray!

There are ruins here, but they're not Indian villages. They're old ranch houses.

CAVE SPEAK

What's with all these cave terms—stalactite, stalagmite, helictite, psue-dospeleoite? Simply put, these are used to describe the general pattern of growth for cave formations. Virtually everything in an active cave "grows" because of two things—minerals in solution and a hole in the ground. The minerals precipitate out of solution onto the walls, ceiling and floor of the cave and how they do this results in the type of spe-leothem they become. Stalactites, as they say, stick tight to the ceiling, while their floor-bound counterparts—the stalagmites—strive mightily to reach them. Helictites seemingly defy gravity and grow up, down and sideways. And psuedospeleoite? That's a term thrown in to confound learned geologists which might be in the audience. It has no meaning at all—I just made it up.

Despite the paucity of petroglyph sites, the single one you'll find here is excellent.

GHOST RANCH

Directions: From Espanola, drive north on US 84 for 37.3 miles to entrance road on the right; it's another 1.2 miles to the museum/visitor center.

Contact Info:
Visitor Information
505-685-1000
www.ghostranch.org

Fee: no fees for just a visit but donations are appreciated

Hours: the Florence Hawley Ellis Museum of Anthropology is open 9 a.m.–5 p.m., Tuesday–Saturday, but closed on Monday; also open 1 p.m.–5 p.m. on Sundays in the summer only

Best time to visit: anytime, whether the weather is weathery or not

Camping/Lodging: rustic lodging on-site; camping at Ghost Ranch and nearby on Carson National Forest land

Access: simple and easy

Jon's Rating: ★★★☆☆ (paleontology)
★★★☆☆ (geology)

Jon's Notes:
Although this area is famous for being the inspiration and backdrop for famous artist Georgia O'Keefe, it is even more important in the world of paleontology as the home to New Mexico's state fossil —*Coelophysis*—one of the earliest known dinosaurs. It and many other important fossils have been excavated from the Triassic "red beds" of Ghost Ranch since the late 1940s. There is a working prep lab in the Ruth Hall Museum of Paleontology and sometimes patrons are allowed to visit excavations. The other great museum here is the Florence Hawley Ellis Museum of Anthropology, with extensive displays of the area's culture, past and present.

LEFT: It's no wonder why famous artists love this landscape.

Geologically, this place is most famous for its abundant fossils.

SHE DID AND SHE DIDN'T

Georgia O'Keefe knew what she wanted, and it wasn't to be stuck in New York City. When she visited New Mexico for the first time in the 1930s, she fell in love with the naked earth-toned buttes and mesas, ultimately buying a house at Ghost Ranch and a place down the road in Abiquiu. Despite her fame and association with Ghost Ranch, O'Keefe never owned the ranch proper, although she did spend a lot of time painting there and became friends with the various owners.

Little guys with an attitude: a pack of Coelophysis on the hunt 215 million years ago.

Artwork by Vernon Morris

Directions: From Silver City, take State Hwy 15 north 44 miles until it ends at the visitor center. Because this road is the ultimate in zigzag rollercoasters, it'll take you 2 hours travel time. Don't even think of going over 25 mph—there are no guardrails. NOTE: If your vehicle is over 20 feet long, you should take Highway 35 through the Mimbres Valley.

Contact Info:
Visitor Information
575-536-9461
www.nps.gov/gicl

Fee: modest day-use fee, but the camping is free—so don't cheat! And how about helping out with a little donation at the visitor center; there's no better cause

Hours: open daily; summer (Memorial Day–Labor Day) 8 a.m.–6 p.m., winter, 9 a.m.–4 p.m.; closed Christmas; the Gila Visitor Center is open every day except Christmas and New Year's

Best time to visit: I love it here best in the fall, with the leaves turning and less crowds; I don't recommend the drive from Silver City in rain and it's a veritable death trap in icy conditions

Camping/Lodging: surprisingly, there's free basic camping in and around the park; you can find improved camping and lodging in Silver City

Access: hike to ruins is an easy to moderate 1 mile round-trip; caution: at the ruins there are exposed drop-offs in some places; keep control of yourself and children!

Jon's Rating: ★★★★☆ (archaeology)

Jon's Notes:
It's a bit of a haul, but once you see this place you'll agree it was more than worth it. The main ruins are up one of the most scenic short hikes you'll ever take in New Mexico. The dwellings themselves are fantastic. The Park Service has improved the place, allowing public access to most of the alcoves, giving you a real feeling for what it was like to live here. There are other treasures in the park too—smaller ruins, pictographs, great trails, and hot springs—plan to spend time in this picturesque setting.

LEFT: One thing's for sure—these cliff dwellers had a fantastic view.

*Here's one way
of making use of
natural alcoves in
a sandstone cliff.*

HIGH-RISE WITH A VIEW

As with other similar dwellings scattered around the Southwest, this area was used by nomadic native cultures for thousands of years before anyone got the idea to set up house way up on a cliff face. Tree ring data indicates the primary cliff-dwelling structures were built around 1280 AD and artifacts identify the culture responsible for the grand architecture as Tularosa Mogollon (pronounced "mo-go-yon"). The name, of course, is a reference to the Tularosa River about 60 miles north where it is presumed the tenants that built and enjoyed this high-rise came from. For whatever reason, the good-old-days here lasted only a few dozen years. It appears everyone moved out around 1300.

The great Indian leader Geronimo was born in this region along the Gila River.
(Artwork by Vernon Morris)

Rock art is in abundance at one point along the Trail to the Past.

WATCH FOR SCORPIONS?

The chances of you seeing a scorpion in this area are pretty slim, especially if you visit in the fall, winter, or spring. So why they have campgrounds named for scorpions, I have no clue. Regardless, be sure to check out the short, 2-part *Trail to the Past* at Lower Scorpion Campground. Up the creek bed from the camp is a small ruin tucked away under an overhang with a couple small pictographs on the wall adjacent to it. Then there is the wall of pictographs with over 80 red images painted along the cliff face. To reach it, follow the paved path behind the toilets (the trail parallels the road) and you'll be there in less than 100 yards, provided the scorpions don't get you.

No, it's not a bad batch of film. That's steam rising from the pools. Hot springs abound in this area. This one– Lightfeather–is only a 20 minute hike from the visitor center.

Directions: Gran Quivira is part of the Salinas Pueblo Missions National Monument. From Mountainair, follow NM 55 south 25 miles. At the right-angle bend, go straight. The parking area is less than a mile ahead on the paved road.

Contact Info:
Visitor Center
505-847-2585
www.nps.gov/sapu

Fee: no fees, donations appreciated; how about building up some good Karma by donating a few greenbacks at the visitor center?

Hours: open daily; summer (Memorial Day–Labor Day) 9 a.m.–6 p.m., winter 9 a.m.–5 p.m.

Best time to visit: this place is especially nice in the fall with the trees in color; avoid midsummer hot spells

Camping/Lodging: camping in Cibola National Forest and lodging in Mountainair

Access: easy paved road to site with easy paths around ruins; much of this is handicap accessible

Jon's Rating: ★★★★✦ (archaeology)

Jon's Info:
Gran Quivira—also called Las Humanas—is the largest pueblo/mission complex of the Pueblo Missions National Monument, at least insofar as excavated ruins are concerned. There are hundreds of rooms, several kivas, and remains of two mission churches here. The site was used off-and-on since at least AD 700, undergoing several major changes in architecture. The visitor center has a nice little museum with an impressive display of pottery, stone tools and other artifacts found at this site. The artisans who lived here were quite adept at carving stone for use as tools and objets d'art. Some stones are carved with faces, while others are made into various effigy shapes, including a mountain lion.

LEFT: Lots of rooms with lots to explore here.

One of the most picturesque ruins in New Mexico, especially in the fall.

LUCKY NUMBER 7

You can't put a square peg into a round hole—or so they say. But you can certainly put a square town over the top of a round one and that's essentially what happened here. In 1967, while excavating Mound 7, archaeologists discovered a curious thing: under the rectangular walls of the current 500 year-old pueblo, there were concentric rows of older, circular walls. Upon further examination they determined that an entire village lay buried below—one that encompassed a giant round kiva some 250 years before.

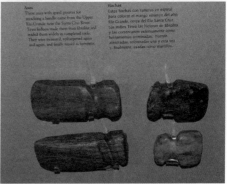

This place has an incredible variety of stone tools and art pieces.

Several kivas abide in these ruins.

BIGGER IS BETTER?

Things at Las Humanas chugged along just fine for a millennia until the Spanish came along in the early 1600s pledging peace, prosperity, and the divine word to the locals. First, they had to have their gigantic church built—with labor conscripted from the Pueblo population. That took the better part of 7 years. Next thing you know, a new friar took over and decided the church wasn't big enough! So, in 1660, he had everyone start work on another, more glorious model. Then, starting in 1665, a drought ensued and people started dying. In 1668 hundreds—perhaps thousands—of people starved to death, but work on the church continued. Suddenly, in 1670 everything abruptly halted. Why? Because everyone left! Needless to say, the second church was never finished.

An artist's rendition of better times at the main pueblo complex.

Artwork by Vernon Morris

Directions: From Los Alamos, take 501 west. In 6 miles it intersects with NM 4. Turn right (west). In another 17.5 miles, a sign for the campground is on the left. Turn left, and after about 0.7 miles more, the campground is on the right.

Contact Info:
Santa Fe National Forest
505-829-3535
www.localhikes.com/Hikes/JemezFalls_0200.asp
www.localhikes.com/Hikes/Jemez_Springs_0200.asp

Fee: camping fee only

Hours: open daily during daytime hours

Best time to visit: fall has the greatest colors and nice temperatures

Camping/Lodging: excellent campground but no hookups; improved camping and lodging at Jemez Springs

Access: easy 0.4 miles (one-way) hike to the falls, moderate to difficult 1.6 mile (one-way) hike to the springs

Jon's Rating: ★★★↗☆☆ (geology)

Jon's Notes:
The walk through the woods to Jemez Falls alone is pleasant enough to warrant a listing in our little book here. And while the cascade on this creek is no Yosemite Falls, it is very picturesque in its own unique way, especially in the middle of winter. McCauley Hot Springs is situated in this ideal setting as well, with several pools of various depths and temperatures. Be sure to check out Soda Dam nearby.

LEFT: It's not Yosemite Falls but it's easier to get to and not nearly as crowded.

Hiking along the Jemez River is especially fun in the fall when the leaves are turning.

McCauley Hot Springs (top) is along this same river and not far away. The trail (left) is pleasant and the wildlife colorful (right).

Directions: Entrance is 1 mile north of Jemez Springs on NM 4.

Contact Info:
Jemez State Monument
575-829-3530
www.nmmonuments.org/inst.php?inst=6

Fee: per person entrance fee; note there is a combination ticket good for admission to both Jemez and Coronado State Monuments for a couple bucks more

Hours: open Wednesday–Monday, 8:30 a.m.–5 p.m.; closed Tuesday

Best time to visit: anytime you can get there is a good time to be there

Camping/Lodging: several campgrounds in area and lodging at Jemez Springs

Access: access is easy with paved trails through the ruins; much of this site is handicap accessible

Jon's Rating: ★★★★☆ (archaeology)

Jon's Notes:
Jemez State Monument encompasses the ruins of a prehistoric village called "Gisewa" as well as the historic San José de los Jemez church that dates from about 1621. Gisewa (the name references the natural springs in the area) may have been the largest pueblo in the region. Not much is left of it today, but it thrived here for two centuries before the Spanish came along. There are educational displays that describe the pueblo and there's even a reconstructed kiva that you can walk through.

LEFT: Once the largest pueblo complex in the region

As usual, the preserved remains of the church dominate what's left of the ruins.

THE CCC CHURCH

The dominant feature in the monument, like many mission/pueblo ruins, is the church. Originally built about 1621, the building was abandoned when the town moved to its present location at Jemez Pueblo a couple of decades later. The church site and surrounding pueblo were first excavated in the early 1920s. Later on, the Civilian Conservation Corps helped to restore much of the building using original materials. The result is what you see today and it's pretty impressive.

The way it may have looked back when the locals were having a rip-roaring good time.

Artwork by Vernon Morris

KASHA-KATUWE TENT ROCKS
NATIONAL MONUMENT

28

Directions: From I-25 at exit 264, south of Santa Fe, head northwest on State Road 16. In 8 miles, turn right onto State Road 22 (there is a sign here for Tent Rocks) and set your odometer to 0.0. In 2 miles you'll cross over the Rio Grande river. At 3 miles turn left, staying on 22. At 4.7 miles 22 ends—turn right onto the paved road past the cemetery. At 5.2 miles the pavement ends at the entrance station. The first trailhead is 4 miles from the entrance.

Contact Info:
BLM Rio Puerco Field Office
505-761-8700
www.nm.blm.gov/recreation/albuquerque/kasha_katuwe.htm

Fee: vehicle entrance fee

Hours: open daily; summer (March 11–October 31) 7 a.m.–7 p.m., winter 8 a.m.–5 p.m.; closed Christmas Eve, Christmas Day and New Year's; last access to the trail is one hour before closing time

Best time to visit: catch it anytime, even in winter after a nice snow, but don't enter the canyon when rain storms are predicted; pay attention to that last warning!

Camping/Lodging: improved camping at Cochiti Lake Recreation Area and lodging in Albuquerque

Access: the Canyon Trail is about 1.5 miles one way; it's easy up through the slot canyon then becomes moderate as you climb to the overlooks above

Jon's Rating: ★★★★✦ (geology)

Jon's Notes:
When was the last time you dropped out of sight and landed in Alice's Wonderland? Here at Kasha-Katuwe Tent Rocks you don't even have to drop acid to do it. This is absolutely one of the greatest treasures of New Mexico—a geologic world altogether wild, weird, and wonderful. The best experience here is the Canyon Trail where you wiggle through a great slot canyon before climbing through the incredible "tent rocks" finally ending at the panoramic overlook. It's one of the best 2-mile (round-trip) hikes you'll ever do.

LEFT: Not your typical stroll in the park

To reach this cool cluster of tent rocks (above) you first have to go through this neat slot canyon (right).

PARTY DOWN WITH THE JEMEZ VOLCANO

The weird tent rock formations found here are a result of a truly wild party that happened in the 'hood about 6-7 million years ago. The Jemez Volcanic Field—a local rock-n-roll club of some loud repute—cranked up the tunes and blasted the whole area with ash, pumice and bits of fractured rock which mixed with super-heated gases in what is known as a pyroclastic flow. The whole thing finally settled and con-gealed but didn't cement together very well. Over the ensuing 6,000 millennia or so, the vagaries of weather wreaked havoc on the hapless sediments, eroding them from the top down. In some cases, a large rock in the upper layers is strong enough to protect sediments below it. The result is a cap worn ever-so-rakishly atop many of the spires.

It's all about geology here, and the geology here is awesome.

LA CIENEGUILLA PETROGLYPHS

29

Directions: From I-25 at exit 276, just west of Santa Fe, take NM 599 northwest. After 2.8 miles, turn left onto Airport Rd. and set your odometer to 0.0. In 2.5 miles Airport Rd. becomes County 56. After 3.4 miles, turn right into the small gravel parking area. The petroglyphs occur along the basalt band on the cliffs in front of you. There are no signs but there are small trail posts with arrows. Follow the well-worn trail to the southwest and then up onto the escarpment.

Contact Info:
575-758-8851
www.blm.gov/nm/st/en/prog/recreation/taos/la_cieneguilla.html

Fee: no fees; here's how you can help: make a donation to New Mexico SiteWatch program via the Archaeological Society of New Mexico www.newmexico-archaeology.org; be sure to label the check "For SiteWatch"

Hours: open during daylight hours

Best time to visit: anytime except in rain; avoid very hot weather—you'll fry out here among the dark boulders

Camping/Lodging: basic camping in nearby Santa Fe National Forest; improved camping and lodging in Santa Fe

Access: trail is of moderate difficulty and winds along the basalt boulders just below the petroglyphs; from the parking area it's a maximum of about 1.3 miles (one-way) to the far end of the site; be careful where you tread so as to not walk on top of any images

Jon's Rating: ★★★★☆ (archaeology)

Jon's Notes:
New Mexico is blessed with a richness of petroglyphs and pictographs—there are great numbers of them scattered all over the state. But the sad fact is you're not gonna see very many because they are either too remote or on private land. Thankfully, here is one of the greatest sites in the rock art world and it's not too hard to get to. As with many such sites, a permanent water source is associated with it—in this case the Santa Fe River. In addition there are pueblo ruins a short distance away that have not yet been extensively excavated. When they are, we may learn a little more about the culture responsible for these images.

LEFT: How many petroglyphs can you see in this photo? Are you sure there aren't more?

If you're not a fan of petroglyphs, you're in the wrong place.

TOTALLY

We were checking out a lead on some petroglyphs north of town but things were looking mighty grim—the little we saw were almost nonexistent. Out of frustration, I stopped and asked a bearded guy jogging along the road. "Man, you are totally in the wrong place!" he declared. "Totally forget about these, man. I mean what you totally want is way over there," he said, pointing west. "Totally?" I asked. "Totally," We went, we saw, and we were blown away by the La Cieneguilla petroglyphs. Totally.

The forms and figures found here are endless.

Directions: From I-25 in Bernalillo, head northwest toward Cuba on US 550. At 21 miles set your odometer to 0.0 and turn left onto Cabezon Road (there's a sign for Ojito). Stay left at the first fork. In about 5 miles, stay right on main road. At about 10.8 miles look for a parking area along Cabezon road on the left. From here, follow the trail north running roughly along the base of the mesa on the left (as of press time there was no parking area here but the BLM intends to build one to service this area). The main hoodoos are about 1 mile from the car.

Contact Info:
BLM Rio Puerco Field Office
505-761-8700
www.nm.blm.gov/recreation/albuquerque/ojito_wsa.htm

Fee: no fees; here's how you can help: make a donation to New Mexico SiteWatch program via the Archaeological Society of New Mexico www.newmexico-archaeology.org; be sure to label the check "For SiteWatch"

Hours: always open, but best in the daytime

Best time to visit: fall–spring is best if the weather is good; even the winter can be nice, but don't head out here in rainy or snowy weather

Camping/Lodging: primitive camping allowed in the wilderness; improved camping and lodging in Albuquerque

Access: moderate to very difficult hiking with no improved trails; bring plenty of water and keep track of your route back

Jon's Rating: ★★★✮✫ (geology)

Jon's Notes:
This is a truly wild area with plenty of wide open country. It's sort of a cross between badlands, desert, and hoodoo-studded galleries of geologic wonder. The scenery here is fantastic, with colorful eroding exposures of Jurassic age (150 million years ago) sediment begging for your attention at nearly every turn. But please watch how you hike around these areas and don't climb any hoodoo—they are prone to collapse and can be dangerous. There are many trails other than the one we list here and they are all worth investigating. Check the website for more information.

LEFT: What's a hoodoo? If you visit this place you'll see plenty of them.

There are strange goings-on in the land of Ojito where cross-bedded sandstones (above) meet tilting hoodoos (right).

PLEASE DO NOT DISTURB

Fossil remains of rare dinosaurs, plants and animals have been discovered in the Ojito Wilderness. They weather out of the 150 million-year-old Morrison Formation, famous for its dinosaurian plenitude. If you happen upon some bones eroding out of a cliff, please do not disturb them (collecting fossils in the Ojito Wilderness is prohibited). Take photos, note the exact location, and call the field office. They'll put you in touch with a paleontologist who will help follow up on your discovery. Who knows —you might even get a dinosaur named after you!

There's lots to see here, including real, live cows. Now there's something to write home about!

ORILLA VERDE RECREATION AREA

Directions: This park runs along a beautiful stretch of the Rio Grande for about 5 miles. From Taos, follow NM 68 southwest about 15 miles to Pilar, then north on NM 570 into Orilla Verde. Petroglyphs abide near Pilar campground, about 1.2 miles from NM 68 and again between the Arroyo Honda and Petaca campgrounds, approximately 3 miles from 68. They also are found along the La Vista Verde Trail, which is about 6 miles from NM 68.

Contact Info:
BLM Taos Field Office
Rio Grande Gorge Visitor Center
575-751-4899

Fee: a modest day-use fee is required per vehicle if you're here for more than 30 minutes

Hours: day use hours are 6 a.m.–10 p.m.

Best time to visit: fall is the nicest time here with all the trees turning color

Camping/Lodging: there's a variety of camping in the park; lodging in Taos

Access: the drive is easy; the hiking is easy to difficult depending on the trail you take

Jon's Rating: ★★★☆☆ (archaeology)
★★★☆☆ (geology)

Jon's Notes:
It's no wonder why this place is so popular, especially in the summer. You can hike in the morning, boat in the afternoon, and fish in the evening. The Rio Grande traces a very scenic path along this stretch, with canyons, buttes, and mesas populating the landscape. This park has a great visitor center, campgrounds, and day-use areas clustered along the banks of the river. Ancient peoples apparently enjoyed the region as well and they left signs of their time here in the form of petroglyphs.

LEFT: Petroglyphs abide along the river here in several places.

If you're not into hiking, bring your kayak.

DESERT VARNISH

In many regions, windborne clay is deposited on sandstone, limestone, or basalt and accumulates on the exterior of the rock. This clay contains additional materials, like iron, and moisture that sustains bacteria, which help produce manganese. For this reason, manganese occurs in high proportions in desert varnish; the darkly-colored manganese is also the source of desert varnish's characteristic coloration. This also makes rocks covered with desert varnish a good medium for petroglyphs. Ancient artisans pecked through the dark surface to reveal the lighter rock below and presto! A petroglyph is born.

This area is one of the most beautiful sections of the famous Rio Grande river.

Directions: Pecos is located about 25 miles east of Santa Fe. From I-25, take exit #299 to Pecos village. Head south 2 miles on Hwy 63 to the park. You can also take exit #307, and head north on Hwy 63 five miles to the park.

Contact Info:
Visitor Information
505-757-7200
www.nps.gov/peco

Fee: per person entrance fee

Hours: open daily; summer (Memorial Day–Labor Day) 8 a.m.–6 p.m., winter 8 a.m.–5 p.m.; closed Christmas and New Year's

Best time to visit: as this area is higher in elevation, it makes for a great destination in the summer, fall and spring

Camping/Lodging: basic camping on Santa Fe National Forest nearby; lodging in Santa Fe

Access: easy hiking on paved trails, most are handicap accessible

Jon's Rating: ★★★★☆ (archaeology)

Jon's Notes:
Just a short drive from the interstate and you can step back in time to any number of time travel destinations. Pecos National Historical Park reveals and protects 12,000 years of history in a single package. There's a lot to learn here with a great selection of sites including the ancient pueblo of Pecos, Spanish colonial missions, a portion of the Santa Fe Trail, a 20th century ranch, and even the site of a Civil War battle. Much of the pueblo and mission have been excavated and are accessible along the walkway. There's even a fully reconstructed kiva which you can enter. And you thought this was just a nice place to picnic.

LEFT: Here's yet another case where the most impressive building in town is the church.

Yes, the colors really do look this intense.

PREHISTORIC BUILDING BOOM

Ideally situated along an ancient trade route, the pueblo of Pecos was well established long before Spaniards entered this country and did their best to ruin the party. First to settle here were pre-pueblo people who lived in pit houses along area drainages about AD 800. But around 1100, some Puebloan architectural entrepreneurs got the idea to build more permanent stone structures. The design was a hit and became quite the building fad over the next few centuries. Some two dozen villages sprouted here, including the one where Pecos pueblo stands today.

If you have to live in a remote area, this one isn't so bad. Even the view is great.

The museum/visitor center houses great collections of artifacts and educational displays.

THE JOKE'S ON YOU

In 1541, Coronado really got carried away with the Conquistador thing. Leading an army of 1,200 he made his way north of Mexico to a cluster of Zuni pueblos near present-day Gallup. He was not welcome, so he attacked the Zuni at Hawikuh, laying waste to the town and taking over the food supply. But 150 miles farther on, at Pecos, the reception was quite different. Indians openly welcomed the soldiers with gifts of food, garments, and local crafts. Alas, that wasn't what Señor Coronado was looking for, so in spring 1541, he set out to find the fabled "Cities of Gold" with his newly-acquired Indian guides. Amazingly, the expedition traveled as far as central Kansas. But riches eluded the deluded Conquistador and, after putting the Indian guides to death for leading him astray, Coronado returned to Mexico a broken and beaten man. The whole thing appears to have been an elaborate and effective ruse put over on the Spaniards by the proud Indians at Pecos. (Artwork by Vernon Morris)

The hustle and bustle of life in the 16th century.

Artwork by Vernon Morris

Directions: Located on the western edge of Albuquerque. From I-40 take exit #154 and head north on Unser Blvd. about 3 miles to the visitor center.

Contact Info:
Park Information
505-899-0205 x331
www.nps.gov/petr

Fee: no fees in most of the park; please donate a few bucks to help out the cause; the City of Albuquerque charges a modest vehicle fee for Boca Negra Canyon

Hours: open daily 8 a.m.–5 p.m.; closed Thanksgiving, Christmas, and New Year's

Best time to visit: fall and winter, when the temperature has cooled down some and the sun is sitting low

Camping/Lodging: camping and lodging in the area of Albuquerque

Access: easy to moderate hikes in and around the lava beds

Jon's Rating: ★★★★☆ (archaeology)
★★★★☆ (geology)

Jon's Notes:
The great thing about Petroglyph National Monument is the fact that it's not buried underneath some shopping center. When you drive around this part of Albuquerque it's wall-to-wall houses, strip malls, chain stores, and monuments to a fast food nation. Thankfully, several years ago, some forward-thinking folks got together and pushed for preserving this incredible treasure. They were successful, and in 1990 the monument was formally established. As a result, some 20,000 petroglyphs and a large amount of unique open space was saved from "lower prices guaranteed!"

LEFT: The variety of petroglyphs found here is astounding.

Most of the petro-
glyphs in the park are
found along the flanks
of ancient lava flows.

THE MAKING OF PETROGLYPHS

Most of the basalt upon which the famous images are inscribed flowed out as lava from a series of volcanic vents that are still apparent to the west. The primary flows that make up the bulk of West Mesa and surrounding landmarks, occurred approximately 150,000 years ago. After cooling and solidifying, the basalt assumed a grayish color. Over the course of many thousands of years, however, iron oxides accumulated on the exposed surfaces, effectively painting the rock with a much darker coating which we call desert varnish. Pecking through the surface creates a stark contrast and a petroglyph is born.

Not only will you find lots of petroglyphs, but you'll also see some great cacti and other native plants.

Directions: From Abiquiu, head southeast on US 84. In 2.4 miles, there will be a sign on the left and a parking area on the right. If you reach the junction with NM 554, you've gone too far.

Contact Info:
no phone
http://en.wikipedia.org/wiki/Poshuouinge

Fee: no fees, but since you're such a nice person and want to do your share to help out, make a donation to the Archaeological Conservancy; contact them at www.americanarchaeology.org

Hours: always open, but you can only see it in the daytime

Best time to visit: you can visit here anytime

Camping/Lodging: basic camping at nearby Santa Fe National Forest, improved camping and lodging in Espanola

Access: easy 0.5 mile one-way hike to the top of the hill overlooking the site

Jon's Rating: ★↗ ★ ★ ★ (archaeology)

Jon's Notes:
I'll admit the name isn't very flattering—Poshuouinge (pronounced 'po-su-in-ge') translates roughly to "Village above the Muddy River." And at first there may not seem to be a lot going for this roadside attraction as compared to other, more-elaborately restored sites in New Mexico. But once you take the trail up to the overlook, you'll see the outline of a huge, impressive, pueblo complex in the valley below. Excavated in 1919, this site was probably occupied by Tewa Indians from about AD 1400–1500. It sure isn't Wally World and that's a good thing.

LEFT: The ruins are not apparent until you hike up the rise—so do it.

PURGATORY CHASM

Directions: From Silver City take NM 15 north toward the Gila Cliff Dwellings. After 25 miles turn right (east) on NM 35. In 4.5 miles you'll see the turnoff for Lake Roberts Picnic Area. The trailhead is on the opposite side of NM 35 across from the picnic area.

Contact Info:
Gila National Forest, Wilderness Ranger District
505-538-2771
www.explorenm.com/hikes/PurgatoryChasm

Fee: no fees, but since you are likely going to the Gila Cliff Dwellings, why not donate something there?

Hours: always open, but best to visit only in the daytime

Best time to visit: good any season but do not attempt during, or just after, heavy rain or snow

Camping/Lodging: camping in the Gila National Forest; lodging in Silver City

Access: easy to moderate hiking through canyons; do not enter the canyon if rain is forecast anywhere in the region; check the weather forecast!

Jon's Rating: ★★ ☆ ☆ ☆ (geology)

Jon's Notes:
We all have our own ideas about what constitutes a "chasm," but after I visited this place, I decided to look up the word in the dictionary. Good old Webster, as usual, has a thing or two to say about "chasm" and roughly says it is "a yawning fissure in the earth's surface." The only yawning here was my own as I searched for what I thought constituted a "chasm" and came up short. Still, on a nice day it's a pleasant enough hike through a bona fide steep-walled canyon, chasm or no chasm. Now don't get me started on the Purgatory thing . . .

LEFT: Maybe not your definition of a bona fide "chasm," but still a neat hike.

Directions: Quarai is part of the Salinas Pueblo Missions National Monument. From Mountainair follow NM 55 north. At 5 miles turn left, following NM 55. After another 2.6 miles turn left onto entrance road. The visitor center is about a mile farther on the paved road.

Contact Info:
Visitor Center
505-847-2585
www.nps.gov/sapu

Fee: no fees, but donations appreciated; how about building up some good Karma by donating a few greenbacks?

Hours: open daily; summer (Memorial Day–Labor Day) 9 a.m.–6 p.m., winter 9 a.m.–5 p.m.

Best time to visit: anytime except when it's really hot in midsummer

Camping/Lodging: camping in Cibola National Forest; lodging in Mountainair

Access: easy paved road to site with easy paths around ruins; much of this is handicap accessible

Jon's Rating: ★★★★☆ (archaeology)

Jon's Notes:
Call me old-fashioned, but I love to see lofty walls of grand old structures reaching to the sky. What's even more impressive is when those walls are hand-hewn sandstone almost 400 years old. The mission church at Quarai is, in my opinion (questionable as it may be), one of the most impressive and beautiful structures in all of the Salinas Missions National Monument. The setting makes it all the more beautiful, especially in the fall when the cottonwood trees turn yellow. There are several huge buildings in various  states of decrepitude that have been stabilized by archaeologists over the last few decades. You are welcome to walk through and among the bulk of them, thanking God you weren't one of the poor souls who had to haul the rocks to make these things.

LEFT: There's a lot of rocks in these walls—be glad you didn't have to carry them!

The most beautiful time here is during the fall when the cottonwood trees turn yellow.

MI CASA, SU CASA

The first blocks of houses were built here around AD 1300. Evidence shows the area was then more-or-less consistently occupied for about a century. For whatever reason, it seems the site was then vacated for almost 200 years. Then, in the late 1500s, the Indians returned and a flurry of new building activity took place. The Spanish came along about that time, saw the primo building site, and decided what the town really needed was a monumental church. The imposing structure was built in the 1620s and used until about 1678 when a severe drought forced everyone to say adios.

The Spanish arrived with a plan for a party—let's build a church!

RED ROCK PARK

Directions: Red Rock Park is just east of Gallup, off I-40 at exit #31.

Contact Info:
505-722-3839
www.ci.gallup.nm.us/rrp/00182_redrock.html

Fee: per vehicle day-use fee

Hours: open daily

Best time to visit: spring and fall are nicest, avoid midsummer heat

Camping/Lodging: improved camping on-site; lodging in Gallup

Access: moderate to difficult hiking trails throughout park

Jon's Rating: ★★★☆☆ (geology)

Jon's Notes:
OK, I've got a problem, I admit it: I'm a serial geophile and I like to watch. Hopefully, now that we're through with the diagnosis, you can understand why I'm attracted to this place (and a lot of New Mexico, for that matter). There's a whole lot of bare-naked geology here and it's just too tempting for an addict such as myself. But the cool thing is you don't need to have a problem such as mine to appreciate the splendiferous landforms and hikes among them. The vibrant colors and subtle textures are so alluring even a computer geek would be turned on. Be sure to stop in at the Red Rock Museum while you're here. They have great cultural collections and a load of information about the local native tribes.

LEFT: Drive off the interstate and step into some cool geology.

Why do they call this place Red Rock anyway? Let's see . . .

DINOSAURS AND SAND DUNES

The spectacular matrix which creates the framework of Red Rock is the result of Jurassic (160 million years ago) sediments laid down during the Age of Dinosaurs (the Mesozoic), although your chances of finding a dinosaur here range from about zero to nil. The Entrada Sandstone forms the bulk of what is seen here today, with exposures consisting of reddish-orange sandy sediments typical of ancient sand dunes. These dunes were deeply buried, cemented, compacted and then raised and eroded to form the massive rock cliffs seen today.

There are miles of hiking trails within the park. But keep track of where you are—it's easy to get lost in the back country.

ROCKHOUND STATE PARK & SPRING CANYON

38

Directions: From Deming, take NM 11 south for 5 miles, and then go east on NM 141 for about 9 miles.

Contact Info:
Visitor Center
505-476-3200
www.emnrd.state.nm.us/PRD/Rockhound.htm

Fee: per vehicle entrance fee

Hours: day use open from 7:30 a.m.–sunset

Best time to visit: nicest in the winter

Camping/Lodging: improved camping on-site; lodging in Deming

Access: easy to moderate hiking, but rock digging can get extreme!

Jon's Rating: ★★★☆☆ (geology)

Jon's Notes:
Once upon a time, in a galaxy far, far away there was a special place rock hounds could go to indulge in their special love for digging in the ground for pretty rocks to take home, polish up and put on the shelf with other family heirlooms. Then word got out and every rock afficionado in the solar system descended on the place and literally scoured it clean. Now it's a quiet, out-of-the-way place to camp and talk shop with others in the geologic world. There's pleasant hiking in Spring Canyon, but don't expect to stock your gem case too full with things you dig up here—there's just not much left. And what is left plays "hard to get."

LEFT: Yeah, there're rocks here, but that's not the only reason to visit. The hiking is rewarding even without carrying home a bag of stones.

SALMON RUINS AND HERITAGE PARK

39

Directions: From US 550 in Bloomfield, head west on US 64. The turnoff to visitor center is 2.0 miles away.

Contact Info:
Park Information
505-632-2013
www.cdarc.org/pages/what/exhibits/visit/salmon.php

Fee: per person entrance fee

Hours: open 8 a.m.–5 p.m., Monday through Friday, 9 a.m.–5 p.m., Saturday and Sunday

Best time to visit: fall is the nicest

Camping/Lodging: improved camping and lodging in the immediate area

Access: easy trails through well-maintained ruins

Jon's Rating: ★★★↗☆ (archaeology)

Jon's Notes:
Salmon Ruins was essentially a Chaco outlier built in the late 11th century along the San Juan River (see also the Casamero Pueblo listing in this book, page 75). There are over 250 rooms here, including various kivas, grain storage structures and generally just about everything you'd need to hang out in the year 1000, including a Whole Foods grocery and boat shops along the river. Recognizing the importance of this site, the local folks and San Juan County Museum Association have done a marvelous job of protecting and interpreting Salmon Ruins for over 30 years. One of the greatest aspects of Heritage Park is its series of replicated habitations including hogans, tepees, and pithouses— many of which you are free to ramble around in.

LEFT: It's amazing what a few dedicated folks can do to preserve some great ruins.

You can hike around and through many of the structures (above) and also see some modern renditions of pictographs (right).

DIGGIN' IT

Salmon Ruins is an admirable collaboration between state, county and local groups who got together with a landowner to preserve a fantastic archaeological site. Originally preserved by homesteader George Salmon and his family, the site and surrounding 22 acres have been owned by San Juan County since 1969. In 1970, the county enlisted professional archaeologists to excavate and stabilize the site. The resulting 10-plus year project was the largest single archaeological investigation ever carried out in the Upper San Juan region. It resulted in recovery of over 1.5 million artifacts and samples, most of which have been preserved and displayed at the on-site museum.

Not everyone lived in classy masonry houses. Some folks kept it simple.

SAN LORENZO CANYON

40

Directions: From Socorro, head north on I-25 about 13 miles to exit 163 at San Acacia. Set your odometer to 0.0 and head south on the east frontage road. At 1.2 miles you pass a one-lane underpass under I-25. At 2.2 miles turn right at the second underpass and go under I-25 heading west. Just after you come out on the west side, the pavement bends south but you go straight onto a dirt road. At 2.7 miles you pass under the power lines. Stay on the main road; do not branch off. At 4.4 miles you will see a sign for San Lorenzo Canyon directing you to turn right. Follow this and stay on the main track. At 7.1 miles you will enter the canyon. If the road conditions are good you can drive all the way to the end, which is another 3/4 of a mile.

Contact Info:
Socorro BLM office
505-954-2115
www.explorenm.com/hikes/SanLorenzo

Fee: no fees; how about donating to Crow Canyon Archaeological Center? Reach them via the web—www.crowcanyon.org

Hours: always open, but best in the daytime

Best time to visit: fall and winter; even if it snows before you get here, it won't stay around very long

Camping/Lodging: basic camping on BLM land; lodging in Socorro

Access: the access road can be impassible for 2 WD cars, especially in bad weather or if the road has not been graded; take a 4WD or call ahead if there's any question; hiking around the floor of the canyon is mostly easy to moderate but can become difficult to extreme if you really get up into the side canyons

Jon's Rating: ★★★★☆ (geology)

Jon's Notes:
It's a little difficult to get to at times, but if you make it you'll be geologically overjoyed. This is one of the nicest hiking areas in the state—with hoodoos, slot canyons, rock shelters, natural arches, and a whole lot of geology going on, but be sure to pay attention to the directions and where you are going. This area is very sandy and you're liable to get stuck if you take a wrong turn. Don't attempt to get out here in bad weather or if the road has not been maintained, especially if you're in a 2WD car.

LEFT: Geology gone wild! They ought to make a TV show out of this.

If you like exploring naked geology, this canyon is one of the nicest hiking areas in the state.

SAN LORENZO-A-GO-GO

The wild rock forms you see here may look like bastard hatchlings of space aliens gone wild or deformed offspring of the Michelin Tire Man but, to be honest, they are not that exotic. Here, again, differential weathering is our friend, attacking the softer, more easily eroded layers more vigorously, undercutting them while the harder ones stand up and out. One last thing, if you're a climber, be aware this rock is notoriously *friable* and does not often afford good protection. Experienced climbers have died here.

Differential weathering is our pal. This is especially true here.

SHIPROCK

41

Directions: The huge monolith rises out of the plain about 12 miles southwest of the town of Shiprock—as the crow flies. Follow US 64 west from Shiprock about 5 miles and turn south on Reservation 571. Drive 8 miles south and you'll be about as close as you can get.

Contact Info:
505-564-7600
www.yellowecho.com/travel/shiprock_nm.htm

Fee: no fee as long as you stay on the road

Hours: always open, but best in the daytime

Best time to visit: anytime

Camping/Lodging: camping and lodging in Farmington

Access: since this is Navajo Nation land you are not allowed to hike around willy-nilly without a permit and a tribal guide

Jon's Rating: ★★★☆☆ (geology)

Jon's Notes:
So, there you are, cruising down the road in northwestern New Mexico, grooving to a little Grateful Dead on the box, kind of zoning out at the boring, flat landscape when you begin to see this "thing' appear on the horizon. As you head south, it looms larger and larger until you can't take your eyes off it. Eventually it has grown so huge, it seems to command the flatlands surrounding it. "What the hell is that thing?" you say to yourself. Shiprock is an 1,800-foot volcanic *monadnock* (look it up in the glossary) that dominates the surrounding land for as far as the eye can see. As you can imagine, it is also a sacred site to the Navajo; they call it *Tse Bi dahi*, or "The Rock with Wings." The name references an old legend that describes how the ancestral Navajo were carried from their place of origin to New Mexico on the back of the "Rock With Wings." Geologically speaking, Shiprock is the remains of a volcano that formed about 30 million years ago. The cinder cone has long since eroded away, leaving behind the more-resistive "neck."

LEFT: The rock that is a ship.

SIMON CANYON RUIN

42

Directions: From Aztec, travel east on NM 173 for about 17.3 miles. Before the bridge you'll turn left onto County 4280 toward Navajo State Park. (NOTE: Do not take 4279 which connects at this same point.) Follow the road 3 miles—past the turn for Navajo SP—where it will end at a gravel parking lot. The marked trail begins in this lot on the far left side. The route leads initially up a fairly steep access road to an active gas well. Once here, you skirt around the fence to the left, following a footpath along the terrace as it runs along the east side of the canyon heading north. The ruin is on this terrace, atop a huge boulder, about 0.8 miles from the parking lot.

Contact Info:
BLM Farmington Field Office
505-954-2000
www.nm.blm.gov/recreation/farmington/simon_canyon_rec_area.htm

Fee: no fees

Hours: always open, but best in the daytime

Best time to visit: whenever the road is passable, which is most of the year; best in the fall

Camping/Lodging: basic camping on BLM land; improved camping at Navajo Reservoir; lodging in Aztec

Access: the road can become impassable in wet weather; the trail has one steep section of moderate difficulty but is otherwise fairly easy; the hike is about 1 mile one-way

Jon's Rating: ★★★☆☆ (archaeology)

Jon's Notes:
When I was a little kid—a year or so ago—I used to march around with my siblings in the wilds of our park-side backyard and establish fiefdoms. Things would go OK until we rightfully demanded taxes from our subjects, who, in a childish effort to usurp our authority, would chase us around the neighborhood. Then we'd retreat to our boulder-top fortress. Simon Canyon Ruin, a Navajo Pueblito, is just such a fort, although it probably wasn't used that way, per se. It seems to be the only "boulder type" defensive site built in this region of the San Juan River. The ruin dates to the mid 1700s and consists of a well-preserved, circular, one-room structure built on top of a large boulder. The amazing thing about this "ruin" is its excellent condition. Over 250 years later the roof is still pretty much intact. It was stabilized in the 1970s and looks like it did the day it was built.

LEFT: A pretty cool boulder-top fort overlooking a scenic canyon. What more do you want?

SITTING BULL FALLS AND CAVE

43

Directions: From Carlsbad, head northwest on highway 285. In about 9 miles, turn left (west) onto NM 137. Continue 24 miles to NM State road 276 and turn right. Follow 276 about 8 miles to its end.

Contact Info:
Lincoln National Forest: 575-434-7200
to reserve a cave visit permit, call the Guadalupe Ranger District 575-885-4181

Fee: modest vehicle parking fee; there is no fee to visit the cave but you *must* reserve a permit 2 weeks in advance by calling the Guadalupe District office; you cannot see the cave without one

Hours: open daily during daylight hours

Best time to visit: the weather here is quite nice in the spring and fall

Camping/Lodging: basic camping on BLM and USFS land; improved camping at Brantley Lake State Park; lodging in Carlsbad

Access: the road is good all the way to Sitting Bull Falls, but 276B to Last Chance Canyon can be rough and impassable for 2WD; trails range from easy to difficult depending on which one and when you do it; the trail to the cave itself is very slippery; however, there is a concrete walkway to the falls overlook that is handicap accessible

Jon's Rating: ★★★★☆ (geology)
★★☆☆☆ (archaeology)

Jon's Notes:
If you're a falling-waters and caves fan then head to Sitting Bull Falls Recreation Area where you'll find a really great day-use area for both. It's not a huge waterfall, but it is pretty unique and in a great setting. The falls flow over an active small limestone cavern and the cave formations are apparent all over the outside. But it's the inside that really is the coolest; stalactites, stalagmites and calcite draperies are jam-packed into the small room. You need a free permit to see this cave—be sure to call 2 weeks ahead. However, there's plenty else that you can do without a permit so you'll not be disappointed even if the trip is on the spur of the moment. This spot is pretty famous so be prepared for crowds on nice weekends. If you want a little more privacy, go to Last Chance Canyon, located nearby—it's got as much or more natural beauty and is another desert oasis.

LEFT: Cave formations on the outside of Sitting Bull Cave.

It's not far from the car and it's pretty easy going to get to the falls.

THE LAST CHANCE

The whole story sounds pretty hokey but it's been told so many times the facts of its origin become a moot point. In the early 1880s a group of local cowboys caught sight of a few Indians and chased them into the wilds. Being the head-strong type with poor navigation skills, they paid more attention to the fleeing suspects than to the route they were on. When the Indians finally shook them off, the cowboys found themselves good and lost among the canyons bordering the Guadalupe Mountains. As the story goes, they became progressively more lost, dehydrated, and desperate as they searched canyon after endless canyon for water. Finally, as they and their horses were about to expire, the desperate ranch hands entered yet another canyon which they figured was their "last chance at salvation." And guess what happened —they all died! OK, OK, just a joke—they didn't die, they found water, and lived to name the canyon.

The approach to Last Chance Canyon. A little harder to get to, but just as fun as Sitting Bull Falls.

Directions: From the Jemez Ranger Station in Jemez Springs, head north on State Highway 4 about 0.75 miles to the pull-off area on the right side of the road.

Contact Info:
Santa Fe National Forest
505-829-3530
www.fs.fed.us/r3/sfe/recreation/districts/jemez/poi/sodadam.html

Fee: no fees except for camping, but since you're such a nice person and want to do your share to help out, make a donation to the Archaeological Conservancy; contact them at www.americanarchaeology.org

Hours: open daily during daylight hours

Best time to visit: anytime you're in the area; day use hours only from 6 a.m.–10 p.m.

Camping/Lodging: campgrounds in area, lodging at Jemez Springs

Access: easy—it's right near the road

Jon's Rating: ★★★☆☆ (geology)

Jon's Notes:
Soda Dam is an accumulation of minerals that have formed at the outflow of a local hot springs. Hydrologic fluids traveling from deep in the earth are overloaded with dissolved minerals as they rise up along a series of local faults in the creekbed. Once they meet the surface, the minerals precipitate out, forming a deposit of travertine. The various colors are a result of iron oxides and trace elements that are trapped in the accreting minerals.

Bubbles seen in the spring waters are mostly carbon dioxide being released from the solution just like those in a can of soda. Soda Dam forms a natural dam to the Jemez River, which cuts through it to continue its course. The unique formation shows the continuous processes of nature, both building and destroying the unique features at the same time.

LEFT: Plop plop, fizz, fizz . . . The gurgling seltzer waters at Soda Dam.

TAOS PUEBLO

45

Directions: The pueblo and museum are just a few miles north of Taos. Follow the signs.

Contact Info:
Taos Pueblo Tourism
575-758-1028
www.taospueblo.com

Fee: per person fee, plus camera/video fees

Hours: open daily 8 a.m.–4:30 p.m. except during times of tribal rituals; in late winter to early spring the Pueblo closes to visitors for about ten weeks

Best time to visit: every season is beautiful here

Camping/Lodging: basic camping at Carson National Forest south of Taos; loads of lodging around the town of Taos

Access: the pueblo usually closes in late winter and early spring as well as during tribal ceremonies; call ahead to make sure it's open

Jon's Rating: ★★★★☆ (archaeology)

Jon's Notes:
If you look at those classic old black and white drawings made of Taos Pueblo in the 1800s, you can just about make out where the artist was standing when the picture was made. That's how little things have changed here. These colorful, multi-storied adobe buildings have been continuously inhabited for over 1,000 years. Taos Pueblo is the only living Native American community designated both a World Heritage Site and a National Historic Landmark. You are welcome to visit the pueblo whenever it is open to visitors, but remember this is a series of private homes and many are not open to the public. Be sure to report to the tourism office beforehand to pay applicable fees and to learn the dos and don'ts.

LEFT: Not your typical view of Taos Pueblo—church ruins and adjacent graveyard.

The church is still a
center of culture here.

TAKE AND GIVE

Taos has its own story of woe due to European expansionism, much of which was thrust upon them by white explorers starting in the 17th century. The persecution carried on into the early 1900s with Congress and President Theodore Roosevelt glomming onto 48,000 acres of traditional Indian lands and turning it into Carson National Forest. Think what you will of "Tricky Dick" Nixon, but in 1970 he did the right thing and returned those lands to the Pueblo of Taos. Not only that, but Nixon included in the repatriation Blue Lake, which the people of the Taos consider sacred due to the spiritual belief that the Taos natives originated from the lake itself. Maybe the beguiling president did deserve his face on a stamp after all.

Taos Pueblo—still keeping it real in the 21st Century.

THREE RIVERS PETROGLYPH SITE

46

Directions: The site is located 17 miles north of Tularosa and 28 miles south of Carrizozo on US 54. Turn east from U.S. 54 at Three Rivers onto County Road B30 and travel 5 miles on the paved road and follow the signs to the site.

Contact Info:
Las Cruces District Office
505-954-2000
www.nm.blm.gov/recreation/las_cruces/three_rivers.htm

Fee: vehicle entrance fee

Hours: open daily; summer (April to October) 8 a.m.–7 p.m., winter 8 a.m.–5 p.m.

Best time to visit: avoid the midsummer heat during the day, this place can be an oven set on "broil;" however, even in the summer, the evenings can be quite pleasant

Camping/Lodging: improved BLM campground next to trailhead; lodging in Tularosa and Carrizozo.

Access: easy access to site; trails are moderate to difficult, especially in bad weather

Jon's Rating: ★★★★☆ (archaeology)

Jon's Notes:
Yeah, sure, you've seen petroglyphs before. Maybe you've seen out-crops where there are zillions of strange, cool etchings. Or perhaps you witnessed some giant painted glyphs hidden among lost canyons. But consider this: whatever you've seen in the world of rock art will not prepare you for Three Rivers Petroglyph Site. It is singularly unique. Not only is the profusion overwhelming, but the creativity is astounding. Subjects span a burgeoning spectrum of real, wild, weird, and abstract imagery. Despite this, the detail is precise, attesting to an artistic acumen that you'll be hard pressed to see elsewhere. Suffice to say your jaw will drop at every other turn, and your idea of artistic boundaries will be thrown out the window.

LEFT: Is there a rock in this photo that doesn't have an image inscribed on it?

One of the world's greatest rock art sites also has some of the most elaborate imagery.

THE MEANING OF LIFE

One man's boulder pile is another man's art studio. And the bigger the pile, the better. After all, it takes a lot of rocks to produce a 21,000 piece petroglyph show. Yet the folks responsible have done a good job of pulling it together here at Three Rivers. The people that created most of these images are known as the Jornada Mogollon, but exactly when they did it cannot be determined. There seem to be several "generations" of etchings, although stylistically most of the figures appear related. What do they mean? Well, they mean whatever you want them to. Unless you can travel back in time to when these were done, and talk to the artists that did them, we'll never know.

Let no rock go unadorned!

Directions: From Albuquerque head south on I-25 to exit #203. Set your odometer to 0.0 and head east on NM 6. In 2.6 miles you'll cross over the Rio Grande. At mile 3.3 turn right on NM 263. At mile 3.9 turn right and head south on NM 47. At mile 6.8 turn left (east) onto Tome Hill Rd. At 7.2 miles the pavement ends. Follow the dirt road to the right and around the south side of the hill. At 7.7 miles, pavement begins again. Make first right onto La Entrada Rd. Pull into the lot with the giant sculptures at Tome Hill Park.

Contact Info:
505-864-6654
www.geocities.com/tomehillnm

Fee: no fees; here's how you can help: make a donation to New Mexico SiteWatch program via the Archaeological Society of New Mexico—www.newmexico-archaeology.org; be sure to label the check "For SiteWatch"

Hours: always open, but best in the daytime

Best time to visit: anytime the weather is good; you cannot easily see the petroglyphs in the rain

Camping/Lodging: improved camping and lodging in Belen

Access: easy drive to base of hill, moderate hiking along basalt outcrop, steep hike up the hill to the crosses

Jon's Rating: ★★★ (archaeology)

Jon's Notes:
Tome Hill pokes its nose up out of the surrounding plains like an inquisitive subterranean giant who wants to sniff the air above ground. This prominent landform has been utilized as a reverential promontory since time immemorial. Early native inhabitants built pueblo structures around its base and carved thousands of petroglyphs along its flanks. Not much is left of the pueblos, but the petroglyphs still abide in the basalt outcrop along the southeastern side of the hill. From Tome Hill Park crosswalk, hike up the paved road about 100 yards and you'll see the basalt band angling up the hill, paralleling the road. Follow the trail below the outcrop and please be careful not to touch the images, they are considered sacred to local natives.

LEFT: The flute player abides in petroglyphs near the base of Tome Hill. There are several dozen images along a short span of basalt.

The park at the base of Tome Hill (above) celebrates all those who pioneered this region—including Indians. Later on, Catholics in the area brought construction supplies to the top and built a monument there (right).

PRAISE FROM ON HIGH

No one knows when, exactly, the first crosses were put up on Tome Hill, but it's safe to assume they weren't installed before the Spanish came along in the 1540s (here's that guy Coronado again). After that, religious priests and devotees sometimes made pilgrimages up the hill to observe high holy days. On other occasions ecclesiastic leaders took to the hill for a birds-eye view and to implore the gods above to influence events below. Sometimes their requests were quite specific. Take, for instance, the story of Father John Ralliere who, in February 1862, reputedly led a flock of choir boys to the top to sing hymns in an effort to aid Union troops who were battling Confederates in the plains below. Apparently it all worked as the friar planned, because the South lost the battle and the war.

Dozens of petroglyphs are found near the hill's base. Evening light is best.

VALLEY OF FIRES RECREATION AREA

Directions: From Carrizozo, head west on US 380 for 4 miles to the entrance on the left.

Contact Info:
Visitor Center
505-648-2241
www.blm.gov/nm/st/en/prog/recreation/roswell/valley_of_fires.html

Fee: there's a vehicle entrance fee based on the number of occupants

Hours: day use area is open daily during daytime hours

Best time to visit: in the fall and winter; avoid midsummer as it can roast you like a hot dog

Camping/Lodging: improved camping on-site; lodging in Carrizozo

Access: nice asphalt road to site with easy paved path through lava beds, handicap accessible

Jon's Rating: ★★★✗ ☆ (geology)

Jon's Notes:
There's no shortage of lava flows in New Mexico. Some old, some (sorta) new. But this is truly one of the best and certainly the only one that's so accessible. There's a paved walkway snaking through the lava with information stations and displays to tell you all about how it happened and why. You need not cry about being trapped on the trail—the friendly management folks allow you to disembark on your own over-lava hike, so long as you are properly outfitted with decent hiking boots and are prepared for some rugged terrain. You'll leave fully educated in the ways of volcanoes and ready for the quiz on Monday.

LEFT: Even the harshness of a new lava flow has beauty springing from it.

It's all about lava. Here you'll learn more than you'll ever remember about it. Good thing there's no quiz . . . or is there?

ACT YOUR AGE

Approximately 5,000 years ago, Little Black Peak got miffed about something and erupted like a volcano (which, incidentally, it was at the time). Its childish spewing-fit created a river of lava that flowed 44 miles into the Tularosa Basin, eventually filling it with basalt. When things settled back down again, the resulting lava flow measured 4 to 6 miles wide and covered an area of about 125 square miles. It's one of the youngest lava flows in the continental United States. This may, or may not, account for its insolent behavior.

The lava field is completely accessible to those with disabilities, with information stations periodically along the walkway.

Directions: The visitor center is located on US Highway 70, 15 miles southwest of Alamogordo.

Contact Info:
Park Information
575-679-2599
www.nps.gov/whsa

Fee: per person entrance fee

Hours: open all year; summer 7 a.m.–10 p.m., winter 7 a.m.–one hour after sunset; visitor center open 8 a.m.–7 p.m. in summer, 8 a.m.–5 p.m. in winter

Best time to visit: in the winter when the sun isn't so harsh

Camping/Lodging: no camping or lodging in park but both are available in Alamogordo

Access: in the winter, when it's cooler, this place is surreal; fall and early spring are also good times

Jon's Rating: ★★★★★ (geology)

Jon's Notes:
One of the things you have to love about America is its sometimes paradoxical dichotomy of a missile or bombing range surrounding a natural wilderness. Long ago the military decided to use the "obviously worthless wasteland" here for rocket, bomb, and ordinance testing, including the detonation of the first nuclear device at what is known as the Trinity Site. Thankfully, some nature-minded savants realized this area for what it is geologically: a unique and specialized desert of gypsum sands unlike any other on the planet. The result is a happy marriage where the popular Moonlight Tour among the dunes has the potential of being cancelled due to missile testing.

LEFT: At last—a gigantic sandbox for adults!

The shifting, whispering sands are sometimes held together by an occasional stalwart yucca.

ERGS ANYONE?

The unique aspect of this environment is not the fact that it is a huge dune field (aka "erg," in the science lingo). After all much of Earth's landforms are made up of sand dunes. Whereas most other sands are primarily quartz or broken down coral or lava, the material that makes up this desert is nearly 100% gypsum. The mineral weathers out of ancient (250 million year old) oceanic sediments trapped in the surrounding mountains and accumulates in playas of the Tularosa Basin. As the shallow lakes evaporate in the dry season, the gypsum is left behind and blown by winds into the dune fields you see here. The location is not out of place, either—many major erg deposits are landlocked. Rather, the rarity of this deposit is in its composition.

The dunes here, as in other places like it, are not static. They are moving almost all the time.

Museums

A:shiwi A:wan Museum

http://ggsc.wnmu.edu/mcf/museums/ashiwi.html
02 E Ojo Caliente Road
P.O. Box 1009
Zuni, New Mexico 87327
505-782-4403

Free—but a donation is greatly appreciated.

Blackwater Draw Museum

www.enmu.edu/services/museums/blackwater-draw/museum.shtml
Eastern New Mexico University
1500 S Ave K
Portales, NM 88130
505-562-1011

Per person entrance fee.

Florence Hawley Ellis Museum of Anthropology

www.ghostranch.org/museums--tours/florence-hawley-ellis-museum-of-anthropology.html
Ghost Ranch Conference Center
US 84
Abiquiu, NM 87510-9601
505-685-4333

Free—but a donation is greatly appreciated.

Haak'u Museum

www.skycity.com
In Acoma at the Sky City Cultural Center
800-747-0181

Per person entrance fee.

Indian Pueblo Cultural Center

www.indianpueblo.org
2401 12th St. NW
Albuquerque, NM 87104
866-855-7902

Las Cruces Museum of Natural History

www.nmculturaltreasures.org/cgi-bin/instview.cgi?_recordnum=CRUC
700 Telshor Blvd.
Las Cruces, NM 88011
505-522-3120

Free

Luna Mimbres Museum

www.deminglunamimbresmuseum.com/HTML/history.html
301 S. Silver
Deming, NM 88030
505-546-2382

Free—but a donation is greatly appreciated.

Maxwell Museum of Anthropology

www.unm.edu/~maxwell
In Albuquerque on the university campus
between Las Lomas and Dr. M. L. King Jr. Ave
505-277-4405

Free—but a donation is greatly appreciated.

Mesalands Community College Dinosaur Museum

www.mesalands.edu/museum/museum.htm
222 East Laughlin Street
Tucumcari, New Mexico 88401
505-461-3466

Per person entrance fee.

The Museum of Archaeology and Material Culture

www.museumarch.org/index.htm
22 Calvary Road
Cedar Crest, New Mexico 87008
505-281-4745

Per person entrance fee.

Museum of Indian Art & Culture

www.miaclab.org
PO Box 2087
Santa Fe, NM 87504-2087
505-476-1250

Per person entrance fee.

New Mexico Museum of Natural History

www.nmnaturalhistory.org
1801 Mountain Road NW
Albuquerque, New Mexico, 87104
505-841-2800

Per person entrance fee.

Ruth Hall Museum of Paleontology

www.nmculturaltreasures.org/cgi-bin/instview.cgi?_recordnum=RUTH
Ghost Ranch Conference Center; US 84
Abiquiu, NM 87510-9601
505-685-4333

Free—but a donation is greatly appreciated.

Wheelwright Museum of the American Indian

www.wheelwright.org
704 Camino Lejo
Santa Fe, NM 87505
800-607-4636

Free

References

Bostwick, Todd W., 2002, *Landscape of the Spirits*, University of Colorado Press, Tucson, CO

Chronic, Halka, 1987, *Roadside Geology of New Mexico*, Mountain Press Publishing, Missoula, MT

Cunkle, James R. and Jacquemain, Markus A., 1996, *Stone Magic of the Ancients*, Golden West Publishers, Phoenix, CO

Ferguson, William M. and Rohn, Arthur H., 1990, *Anasazi Ruins of the Southwest in Color*, University of New Mexico Press, Albuquerque, NM

Knopper, Steve, *2006 Moon Handbooks—New Mexico*, Avalon Travel Publishing, Emeryville, CA

Noble, David Grant, 2000, *Ancient Ruins of the Southwest*, Northland Publishing, Flagstaff, CO

Malotki, Ekkehart and Weaver, Donald E., 2002, *Stone Chisel and Yucca Brush*, Kiva Publishing, Walnut, CA

McCreery, Patricia and Malotki, Ekkehart, 1994, *Tapamveni*, Petrified Forest Museum Association, Petrified Forest, CO

Websites

Government websites:
www.nps.gov
www.fs.fed.us
www.LNT.org
www.nm.blm.gov
www.newmexico.org
www.fs.fed.us/r2/recreation/Heritage/index.shtml

Other non-commercial websites:
www.explorenm.com
www.localhikes.com
www.centerfordesertarchaeology.org
www.americansouthwest.net/new_mexico/index.shtml
http://rockart.esmartweb.com
www.sidecanyon.com

GLOSSARY

anthropomorph OK I admit this sounds a bit out there but here goes: Anthropomorphs are rock art images which resemble human forms, at least a little. Some folks think they're more likely space aliens which could account for the many strange appendages and ornamentations often found within these images. Not to mention the sudden disappearance of guidebook authors at such sites.

archaeology Why are you asking me this? You should know it already! It's basically the study of ancient cultures, their remains, artifacts, structures, and influences.

Archaic In North America, the native cultures which predate the ancestral pueblo peoples but occur after Clovis time. The Archaic period is roughly defined as running from about 6,000 BC to about 900 BC.

basalt The most common type of lava. Composed mostly of fine crystals of feldspars and olivine.

cenote Small perennial lakes trapped within steep-walled sinkholes that extend below the water table.

Clovis Primarily refers to a distinct form of stone tool manufacturing. Clovis points are fundamentally more refined and advanced than previously fabricated tools. The term also, more loosely, defines cultures that fall within a temporal context after Paleo-Indians but predating Archaic. Generally considered from about 10,000–6,000 years BC.

column Geologically speaking it refers to a pillar of rock. In caves it refers particularly to a speleothem that forms when a stalactite eventually connects with its corresponding stalagmite. The whole cavern has a huge party whenever this happens.

desert patina / desert varnish The effect is as if some cosmic woodworker spilled a very large bucket of dark stain over the desert floor, coating all the exposed rock on the surface. That stain is comprised mostly of iron oxides that color the outer surface dark brown to black, while the inside is the natural rock color, usually much lighter. Recent research shows that desert varnish is primarily a result of biochemical processes.

friable Has nothing to do with frying anything. Unless, of course, you're taking illicit drugs which fry your brain cells and compel you to climb rock which bears this description. Friable refers to rock which flakes and crumbles easily—not the kind of thing a sensible and sober climber would attempt to scale.

eye Here I take the easy way out and telling you to go look up the term "window" which, lucky for you, actually is defined later in the glossary.

geode Another one of those cool geologic terms that you can throw around at dinner parties and impress dignitaries with. Refers to crystal-lined cavities in rock.

geoglyph A singularly cool archeological site made by either aligning/piling rocks into designs and shapes, or, alternatively, by deliberate removal of stones from an area creating recognizable patterns in the ground during the process.

geology A very cool and hip career if you can make a living at it, which most geology graduates have a hard time doing. The term refers to the study of the Earth and the processes that continue to shape it.

helictite One of the stranger cave formations. Helictites obviously have no respect for gravity and grow at improbable angles up, down, and sideways. These formations build up as a result of micropressures, seemingly defying gravity.

Hephaestus The ancient Greek god of fire, son of Zeus and Hera. Probably not someone you'd want to tick off. Apparently likes hanging around volcanoes.

Hisatsinom A somewhat loosely-defined group which primarily refers to ancestral Hopi. The Hisatsinom had their start as a recognizable group about 900 BC, just after the Archaic.

hoodoo I do, you do, we do... Hoodoos! Refers to strange-shaped pillars of rock, bent and gnarled by erosion and often capped by a large slab of harder rock which protects the softer layers below. Generally composed of easily-eroded sandstone or claystone.

karst Here we go again with those wacky geologic terms. Karst refers to landforms characterized by surface sinkholes, ravines, depressions and, most of all, subterranean cavities (caves). Karst usually forms in areas of high calcium and gypsum rock such as limestone and marble which are easily eroded by water solutions traveling through it. The term comes from a limestone plateau by the same name near Trieste, Italy where this phenomenon is especially apparent.

lava You should know this already, but here's a little more info for ya: Yes, we all know this is volcanic in origin. But lava need not have come from a stereotypical volcano. It often arrives by out-pouring from large cracks in the Earth's crust.

lava tube A natural 'tube' that forms when a lava 'river' exits from a sub-surface channel in a lava flow, leaving a roofed-over tunnel in its place. In highly volcanic areas lava tubes are often very abundant.

Leave No Trace A code to live by when traveling through the wild— don't disturb wildlife or collect anything except memories and photos. Try to leave nothing behind; in fact, we suggest going a little further by picking up trash whenever you see it. The Great Spirit appreciates those who help out Mother Earth.

lithology Refers to rock. And I don't mean rock-and-roll bands. Rather it's all about stony rock—the different types, their composition, and the processes that produce them. Also can mean the subdivision of geology which studies rock.

magma Molten rock or lava before it has cooled. Don't touch it.

metate Stone grinding surface used by native cultures to pulverize corn and other plant material.

monadnock Mona what? How someone came up with this baby I'll never know. But, it is real and does mean something, at least to someone. It's a geologic term which refers to a giant rock-form that loftily protrudes above its flat surroundings.

Paleo-Indian Term given to all ancestral Indians that predate well-documented dominant native cultures. In North America this generally refers to any pre-Clovis peoples older than about 8,000 years.

paleontology The study of fossils, which, in turn, has nothing to do with the watch-making company of the same name. To become a paleontologist is to seek a blissful torture.

petroglyph Petro means rock, glyph means form. Can you add them and come up with something other than "rock form?" This term also references the way in which the image is made—etched or inscribed into the rock face by pecking away the outer surface.

pictograph Meaningful painting on rocks by ancient cultures. (As opposed to meaningless painting on subway cars, which we scientists call "graffiti.")

pueblo Do I really need to spell this out for you? OK, OK it's a term used to denote a communal building structure that generally houses multiple families and is the center of activity for a given community.

rift One of those things that sometimes ruins a relationship, often forming as a result of two parties, once inseparable, going divergent ways. It happens with people and it happens with rocks the same way.

riparian Has nothing to do with repairing anything. Refers to natural environments that abide along permanent waterways. Home to wildlife galore.

selective weathering/selective erosion The key here is "selective"—like "selective service" when Uncle Sam calls you up for military duty. Certain rocks are softer than others and erode away much faster, leaving the harder, more durable, rock to stand out like a Marine Special Forces recruit in a monastery.

sink If you're thinking of the catchment basins in your house then you're not too far off. Now imagine a depression in the ground which effectively performs similarly to your kitchen sink and you've got it.

slot canyon a.k.a. "slot," a term which pretty well describes what it means—a narrow, steep-walled canyon. Some slots are only a few feet wide but have walls hundreds of feet high. Stay out of these if rain is predicted anywhere in the region.

speleothem A sufficiently provincial subterranean-geology term that refers to any depositional structure commonly found inside limestone caves. Synonymous with "cave formation." There are lots of these in active limestone caves. They take a long time to grow, so please keep your hands off them.

stalactite A common speleothem which grows from the ceiling of caves. Stalactites "hold tight" to the ceiling and grow down toward the floor.

stalagmite Counterpart to stalactites, a speleothem that grows from the floor up toward the ceiling. Stalagmites "might" reach the ceiling.

tree ring dating You're probably astute enough to know this phrase isn't hinting at a romantic night out between two annular growths of tall woody plants, but what you may not know is that it refers to an absolute method of dating ruins which contain preserved tree parts in their structure. By looking at the patterns in the annular rings, researchers are often able to match them precisely with known records of tree growth, thereby pinpointing the years the tree was alive.

volcanic bomb It's not something likely to turn up in Transportation Safety Administration (TSA) checks of luggage at the airports, but you never know. When a volcano explodes and hurls liquid magma skyward, the globs cool and harden as they fly through the air, developing tell-tale shapes before hitting the ground or clueless bystanders.

tuff Sometimes it is and sometimes it isn't—tough, that is. It all depends on how it was deposited and what's happened to it since. Tuff is a volcanic rock made up primarily of consolidated ash spewed out of a volcanic vent. It's stable, yet workable, nature makes it an attractive building material in many places throughout the world.

window If you had a solid wall on your house that you wanted to let the sun shine through, what would you do? Smash a hole in the sucker, of course. That bit of handiwork is called a window. Now let me ask you, why should Mother Nature shy away from doing the same thing when she wants to have sunlight stream through a hard rock wall?

INDEX

Abiquiu 121, 169, 220, 222
Abo Ruin 25, 26, 27
Acoma Pueblo (Sky City) 29–31
Alamogordo 217
Albuquerque 3, 14–15, 29, 143, 151, 165, 209, 221–223
Angel Peak Scenic Area 33–35
animals 14, 20, 39, 153
anthropomorph 224
archaeology 12, 16, 22, 25, 29, 37, 41, 45, 55, 75, 81, 99, 105, 111, 115, 123, 129, 139,
    147, 151, 155, 159, 165, 169, 173, 183, 193, 195, 201, 205, 209, 224
Archaic 224–225
Aztec 37–39, 41–43, 193
Aztec Arches 37–39
Aztec Ruins National Monument 41–43

Bandelier National Monument 6, 45, 46–49
Bandera Volcano and Ice Cave 51
Bernalillo 151
Bisti/De-Na-Zin Wilderness 55–57
Bloomfield 33, 81, 183
Blue Hole 59
Bottomless Lakes State Park 61–63

Capulin 16, 65–67
Capulin Volcano National Monument 65–67
Carlsbad 5, 8, 23, 69–73, 195
Carlsbad Caverns National Park 5, 8, 23, 69–73
Carrizozo 205, 213
Casamero Pueblo Ruins 75
Catwalk National Scenic Trail 77–79
cenote 224
Chaco Culture National Historical Park 5, 22, 81–87
City of Rocks State Park 89–91
Clayton 5, 22, 93–97
Clayton Lake State Park 5, 22, 93–97
Clovis 224, 226
column 224
Coronado State Monument 99–101
Cuba 151

Deming 89, 181, 221
desert 18, 21, 59, 151, 157, 167, 195, 217, 219, 224
desert patina / desert varnish 157, 224
dinosaurs 14, 22, 35, 93, 95, 119, 153
dunes 219

Echo Amphitheater 103
El Malpais National Monument 105–109
El Morro National Monument 111–113
ergs 219
erosion 57, 106, 226
Espanola 103, 119, 169
eye 19, 21, 89, 93, 191, 211, 225

Farmington 33, 55, 191, 193
Fort Stanton Recreation Area 115–117
fossils 14, 15, 22, 119, 120, 153, 226, 232
friable 46, 189, 224

Gallup 163, 177
geode 225
geoglyph 225
Geronimo 125
Ghost Ranch 103, 119–121, 220, 222
Gila Cliff Dwellings National Monument 123
Glenwood 77
Gran Quivira 129–133
Grants 51, 75, 105, 106, 111
gypsum 217, 219

Hephaestus 225
Hisatsinom 224–225
hoodoo 57, 151, 225

Jemez Falls and McCauley Hot Springs 135–137
Jemez Springs 135, 139, 199
Jemez State Monument 139

Kasha-Katuwe Tent Rocks National Monument 143

La Cieneguilla Petroglyphs 2, 147, 148–149
lava 35, 79, 105, 107–109, 165–167, 213–215, 219, 224, 225, 226
lava tube 225
Leave No Trace 18, 57, 225
lithology 226
Los Alamos 45, 135

magma 226–227
metate 226
monadnock 191, 226
Mountainair 25, 129, 173
museums 4–5, 11, 220

Ojito Wilderness 14, 55, 151–153
Orilla Verde Recreation Area 155–157

Paleo-Indian 226
Paleontology 4–5, 11, 14, 22, 119, 222
Pecos 2, 13, 61, 63, 159, 160–163
Pecos National Historical Park 2, 159–163
petroglyph 25, 117, 157, 167, 207, 226
Petroglyph National Monument 165–167
pictograph 226
Poshuouinge Ruins 169
pueblo 41, 43, 111, 129, 131, 133, 139, 141, 147, 159, 161, 169, 201, 203, 209, 224, 226
Purgatory Chasm 171

Quarai Ruin 173–175

Red Rock Park 177
rift 15, 226
riparian 226
Rockhound State Park & Spring Canyon 181
Roswell 61, 115
Ruidoso 115

Salmon Ruins and Heritage Park 183–185
San Acacia 187
San Lorenzo Canyon 7, 187–189
Santa Fe 135, 147, 159, 169, 199, 222
Santa Rosa 59
selective weathering/selective erosion 226
Shiprock 191
Silver City 77, 89, 91, 123, 171
Simon Canyon Ruin 37, 193
sink 61, 227
Sitting Bull Falls and Cave 195–197
Socorro 187
Soda Dam 135, 199
speleothem 117, 224, 227
stalactite 117, 224, 227
stalagmite 73, 117, 224, 227

Taos 6, 155, 201–203
Taos Pueblo 201–203
Three Rivers Petroglyph Site 205–207
Tome Hill 209–211
tree ring dating 227

tuff 45–46, 49, 227
Tularosa 125, 205, 215, 219

Valley of Fires Recreation Area 213–215
volcanic bomb 227

White Rock 45
White Sands National Monument 217–219
Whites City 69
window 205, 225, 227

ABOUT THE AUTHORS

Jon Kramer is an adventurer first, and also a geologist, writer, climber and surfer (but not necessarily in that order, depending on the surf). He received his Bachelor of Science degree in geology at the University of Maryland and has pursued life as an adventuring paleontologist ever since. His interests are quite varied and include all things natural. In addition to popular travel and adventure writing, Jon has published scientific papers on critters as ancient as 2 billion-year-old bacteria and as young as 12,000-year-old mammoths. Jon travels extensively with his wife Julie, sometimes settling down for a rest in Minnesota, Florida, California and interesting points in between.

Julie Martinez is an explorer, naturalist, freelance artist and formal art instructor. Her appreciation for insects, plants, rocks and fossils started in childhood with a collection that has grown throughout her life. Julie graduated from the University of Wisconsin, Stevens Point, with a degree in Fine Arts and Biology. She initially worked as an illustrator for the medical field but in the late 1980s began a freelance career, which she has enjoyed ever since. Julie's work is featured in many textbooks, journals and museum exhibits throughout North America. She is also a staff teacher at Minnesota School of Botanical Art. When not teaching, she travels with Jon, exploring the wilds of the world.

Vernon Morris is a freelance artist, muralist and adventuring time traveler. His formal art education took place in the early 1980s at the University of Minnesota and Minneapolis College of Art and Design. Vern's Native American (Anishinabe) roots have been a powerful influence in his life. He maintains a small quarry at Pipestone National Monument where he excavates the famous carving stone every year. He then sculpts it into pipes and ritual objects just as his ancestors did for countless generations. Vern carries his work with him into the wilds and is just as comfortable carving pipestone atop a mesa in the Southwest as sketching scenes from antiquity along the ocean in Big Sur.